BILLY BRAGG

Midnights in Moscow

BY CHRIS SALEWICZ

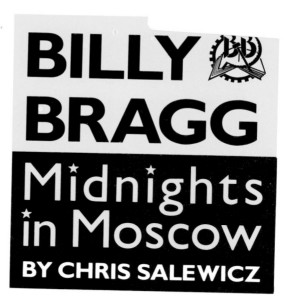

WITH PHOTOGRAPHS BY ADRIAN BOOT

Omnibus Press

London/New York/Sydney/Cologne

© Copyright 1989 Omnibus Press
(A Division of Book Sales Limited)

Edited by Chris Charlesworth
A Thumbnail Design. Assisted by Tony Benn
Picture research by Debbie Dorman/Adrian Boot
Project/typesetting co-ordinated by Caroline Watson
Typeset by Capital Setters, London
Printed by The Eagle Press plc, Blantyre, Glasgow, Scotland
For support on the field, above and beyond the call of nature:
Wiggy, Billy Bragg, Peter Jenner (for rewrites and
distributions of profits), Vivien Goldman, everyone involved
with conscientious delays during the course of this book, Sumi
Jenner, the KGB and, last but not least, Mikhail Gorbachev.

Picture credits:
All photographs by Adrian Boot except:
Bragg Collection: P7, 10(t), 12, 14, 80(t).
Jayne Creamer: P8, 10(b), 13, 22.
Contemporary/NFA: P45.
The Hulton Picture Company: P53.
Novosti Press Agency: P25, 34, 51(b), 53, 84, 86.
A. Shterenberg: P36 (Mayakovsky).
Paul Slattery: P16, 20(b).
Wiggy: P19, 20(t).

ISBN: 0.7119.1670.5
Order No: OP44973

Exclusive distributors:
Book Sales Limited
8/9 Frith Street,
London W1V 5TZ, UK

Music Sales Corporation
225 Park Avenue South,
New York, NY 10003, USA

Music Sales Pty. Limited
120 Rothschild Avenue,
Rosebery, NSW 2018, Australia

To the Music Trade only:
Music Sales Limited
8/9 Frith Street,
London W1V 5TZ, UK

 BILLY BRAGG

The opening 14 notes of the tune 'Midnight In Moscow' seemed to permeate every nook and cranny of the Ukrainia Hotel. Played somnambulantly on some kind of glockenspiel, and followed by sombre tones spoken in Russian, it was the call sign of that snappy, poppy, go get 'em station Radio Moscow.

Midnight in Moscow was a special time for us. After our Russian hosts had departed and everywhere interesting was closed for the night, we would gather together in someone's room and reflect. Sharing a bottle of pepper vodka liberated from the hard currency shop (Wiggy says all foreign currencies are hard), we would discuss our experiences of the day and how this affected our preconceptions of the Soviet Union. After a while, and a few pepper vodkas, amazement would give way to exhaustion and one by one we would depart to wander the cavernous corridors of the Ukrainia in search of our overheated rooms and cosy beds. Morning in Moscow I found as difficult as anywhere else but after a deep, hot bath with a cup of herbal tea and some Van Morrison on the Walkman, I was ready for another day of eye-opening experiences on the streets of Moscow.

Having now explained the title of this book to you, I feel duty bound to state that it was not my first choice. Looking at all the photographs to be included, I felt that a better title would have been *Billy Bragg wears lots of funny hats in the Soviet Union*. I took to wearing whatever hat I could lay my hands on for two reasons. Firstly, it was very cold, and secondly everyone in Moscow wore one. In staid Britain you really need a good excuse to wear a hat, like being a fireman or a person who listens to jazz records. In the Soviet Union not wearing a hat in the Moscow winter points you out immediately as a foreigner. And a lunatic.

As more and more Western musicians perform in the Soviet Union, the question arises as to which are doing it for crass publicity purposes and which are committed to the process of breaking down the cultural barriers that exist between East and West. There is a simple way to tell the difference. The next time a band returns from Moscow with a video shot in Red Square don't ask them the usual Cold War questions. Ask them when are they going back?

INTRODUCTION BY BILLY BRAGG

BILLY BRAGG/A BRIEF OUTLINE

SCHOOL'S OUT

Billy Bragg and his best friend and next door neighbour Wiggy, went to Northbury Junior School, the same school their fathers had gone to. Also, like their fathers they went to Park Secondary Modern, later one of the new comprehensive schools. They even lived in the same houses their dads had lived in when they were kids, the only difference being that their families had swapped houses in the thirties.

Life was pretty well pre-ordained in the structured world of Barking in the sixties. Fords and the docks were the two main employment opportunities, with their associated firms, and the small service jobs being the main alternative. Success was moving out to the semi-rural suburb of Loughton, and professional advancement was becoming a foreman, though even this raised problems. But it was also a secure and stable existence, and the welfare state and the steady growth of the fifties and sixties had removed most of the uncertainties and insecurities of the thirties.

The most exciting time of the year was Christmas when all the family would get together at his grandmother's house. Billy's mother, also from an East End background, had five sisters and a brother, all of whom had kids, and it would not

be unusual for a dozen children to be around on Christmas Day. Family and Barking were the important parts of growing up. Listening to his father reading from Kipling, not the jingoist stories but the English poems. His father also told him tales about his time in India with the Armoured Corps when he was conscripted into the Army 'for the duration', which turned out to be from 1942 until 1947, leaving just before Independence. A distant and exotic experience that had excited and stimulated the father as much as the son. It was his father who also stimulated his love of football, and his so often frustrating support of West Ham.

One of his earliest memories was of England winning the World Cup in 1966. "My Mum was ironing, and she said, 'Oh, those poor Germans', while me and my Dad looked at each other incredulously, we just couldn't understand. Then he said, 'You must come with me, you'll never see this again.' He took me out into the street, on the incredibly busy road to Ilford, and – there was nobody there. 'You'll never see this again – short of there being a World War.' It was very spooky."

School however was a bore that had to be endured. Not much was expected, and not much was achieved. As long as you were capable of going on to the production line at Fords in Dagenham the school had done its job. No one ever went to University or any other advanced higher education; that was for the kids from the Grammar School. The merging of the Grammar School with the Secondary Modern into the Comprehensive School had no immediate effect, merely bringing the two rival factions closer to each other and enabling the aggravation between them to occur at closer range.

English was the exception to this. Billy won a poetry prize in his first year and even got to read his work on the local radio station, having first

convinced the teachers that he had written it himself and not pinched it from some obscure source.

School also introduced Billy to racism and fascism. The Fascist newspaper *Bulldog* was sold outside the school gates, and petty harassment of Sikhs for wearing turbans and being different was routine.

"There was hostility from a group of kids – tough nuts – who'd get fun out of knocking off Indian kids' turbans. At the time I thought it was really out of hand, but I never did anything to say that's racist crap. It didn't occur to me that it was anything other than spiteful, and there was that terrible feeling – rather them than me. If there wasn't them, and those Grammar School kids, then it would have been me. And eventually, it was.

"It might have been that I'd started playing the guitar, but near the end of school, I transgressed an unwritten law, upset the hooligan faction, and got kicked in the chops a couple of times. I never told my parents – there was nothing anyone could do, I just said fuck it. It was only the last six months, when I was 16.

"There was also a real sense of pointlessness about going to school, 'cos I knew that as soon as I left, I'd buy a suit, and get a job. Which was exactly what I did. No one ever asked me what qualifications I had. I got a grade A in my English Language O-Level, so I thought it was a piece of piss, I'll just knock 'em out; but when I failed all the

others, it was a real shock to my parents. I'm just no good at exams, I go to pieces on the day; I failed my driving test three times. I've always been against the idea that your entire scholastic career should depend on what happens on one particular afternoon."

Billy did not play in any bands at school, although there were a couple of heavy metal bands there. His tastes were initially more towards T.Rex and Slade, graduating to David Bowie ('Aladdin Sane'), and Elton John ('Yellow Brick Road'), and above all Rod Stewart And The Faces – real East End heroes.

"When 'Tubular Bells' by Mike Oldfield came out there was another big split. We all listened to it at home with the lights out. We didn't smoke dope though, it was the Grammar School boys that did that, so we didn't want anything to do with it. Our thing was pills for keeping you awake all weekend, but mostly we were all fuelled on 'Party Sevens' of Double Diamond, huge cans of cheap beer."

But it was Bob Dylan, Motown, and reggae that really made a big impression. "I'll always remember the first time I heard Bob Marley. The song was 'Concrete Jungle', and I thought, that's incredible! Desmond Dekker with guitar solos, it's so great!"

Unable to play guitar, but having whetted his appetite for words with his poems, Billy wrote songs and memorised tunes to go with them. Wiggy was living next door and, as always, Billy could hear him practising through the wall. Eventually in the summer of 1974 he started teaching Billy how to play.

"In my branch of the family there wasn't even a record player, and no one could play. But my mother's side of the family were liable to break into song at the least excuse, led by my grandmother who played a variety of old music hall tunes on the piano at Christmas. My mum's sisters

could play as well, and an uncle played in a dinner-dance band, and another played Parker-esque saxophone in his spare time."

In 1974, Billy's father took him to Nathaniel Berry, the piano dealers in Ripple Road, Barking, and bought him his first guitar, a Spanish-style acoustic for £16.00.

Leaving school that same summer was a bit of an anticlimax, and after an unbearable six months working for Overseas Containers Ltd in their insurance claims department, he left, much to the chagrin of his parents.

"I went to France for the summer of 1975, to hitch hike around. With my pack on my back and £100 in my pocket, off I went down the West Coast, across to the Mediterranean and then to Menton on the Italian border. I slept on the beach, and really lived the part – it was the gypsy in my soul! Any time I got hold of a guitar, I'd be singing songs like 'Me And Bobby McGee' (like Janis Joplin). It went on till I ran short of money and had to go home. I never did get to Rome as I'd planned."

Billy arrived home just as his father went into hospital with cancer of the lung. Within 18 months, in October 1976, he died aged 52. Billy had always been very close to his dad, and watching him die was a harrowing experience. "He'd smoked like a chimney for 40 years and never had a day's illness, and then one day he just began to wither away."

GARAGELAND

1976 was not only the year when the 19-year-old Billy's father died but it was also the year of punk and the 19-year-old Johnny Rotten. Billy and Wiggy though, were into The Rolling Stones ('Black And Blue' was a particular favourite), and Bob Marley's 'Natty Dread'. In his mum's back room they were getting into 'Exile On Main Street', 'Let It Bleed', Chuck Berry and lots of early rhythm 'n' blues based songs.

"When I heard the first Damned album, I thought, forget it, I can't get into this. Being in East London we might as well have been living on the moon. Heavy metal was the only live music in the pubs round our way. You had to go to the West End or West London to hear punk and I didn't like going up there, it all felt uncomfortable.

"Mod was something I could tune into more than the safety pin through the nose business. The Sex Pistols always had Art School stamped all over them as far as I could see. It might have been just our stupid prejudice, but The Jam seemed both working-class and stylish. This was during the 'fire and skill' period (that's what Weller had written on his amp) and we used to see them play at the Nashville – they were brilliant.

"We went to see The Jam play at the Rainbow in Finsbury Park, and it was the first night of The Clash's White Riot Tour, with The Subway Sect who were dreadful, and The Buzzcocks, who still had Garth playing bass. The gig was too big for The Jam, they didn't seem to have the same energy as they had at the Nashville. But it was a revelation when The Clash came on. For me and Wiggy it was like St. Paul's experience on the road to Damascus.

"They seemed to be doing everything we liked about The Rolling Stones, but they were our age. On the way out of the gig we decided that was that . . . we were going to be like The Clash, with all that energy, all those guitars, but not relying on over-playing and guitar solos. It was rock 'n' roll but suddenly it was us. It was here, it was our age. It wasn't about driving around America in limos with hundreds of roadies, it was within reach. I hated ELP, Queen and all those types of groups. It was the Cultural Revolution, the Youth Millennium for my generation, and The

Clash seemed to sum it all up.

"After that gig it was haircuts all round, and all the Lionel Blairs (flared trousers) were out the window."

Inspired by this experience, Wiggy and Billy got together with Robert Handley, a drummer who also lived in their street and formed a band. They rehearsed every Friday night in Gascoigne School, an old school building that resembled a Victorian workhouse, in a little room with egg boxes stuck all over the walls and ceiling. Otherwise they'd go out to a building on the A13 (the local main highway), past Ford's along the river, and stay up all Saturday night, playing every song they knew, from the blues to The Clash, via Chuck Berry, The Stones, The Faces, Motown and r'n'b standards, with the odd reggae song thrown in for good measure.

"I was writing songs too, so we'd do a few of mine. By this time I was out of my Jackson Browne period, because I'd discovered the man who gave me what Jackson had, but with a backbeat, and he was from my world – Elvis Costello. He taught me that singer/songwriters didn't have to be self indulgent, that they should be provocative."

But there were no gigs, the only local pub with live music was The Bridge House at Canning Town, and that was all heavy metal where Def Leppard and Iron Maiden were particular favourites.

In the summer of 1978 they all decided to go on holiday together, somewhere where they could play guitars, get drunk, and stay up all night. After dismissing Butlins, they saw an advert in *Melody Maker* for a rehearsal studio in the country, so they rang up and negotiated a special rate for two weeks.

"It was amazing. We did everything we'd ever wanted to do – stayed up as late as we liked, played our guitars as loudly as we wanted to, got drunk as lords, and met girls. We never really came home. Obviously, we did physically, but we started going up there every weekend. By the start of the New Year we decided to give up our jobs, and in April started to live up there in Oundle, just outside Peterborough."

The rehearsal room was run by Ruan O'Lochlain and his wife Jackie. Ruan was a musician who played with Ronnie Lane's Slim Chance, the pub rock band Bees Make Honey and various other name and semi-name bands. He was the first professional musician they had met, and with his and Jackie's help they chose the name Riff Raff, started gigging, and subsequently even made several singles. Their first gig was at The Bull, in Irthlingborough, near Kettering, and they even

Left: Early Riff Raff-top Robert, bottom left Wiggy, Kevin, Billy.
Above: Riff Raff at Gladstone Arms, Peterborough, Easter 1981.

secured a support spot at the Marquee a couple of weekends after that.

They stayed up there all that summer of 1979, first living in a farmhouse, then lodging with a local family who had a large house. After completely disrupting family life for a couple of months, they were thrown out and re-housed in a one-up, one-down, and one-in-the-middle, house in the centre of Oundle. The house was nicknamed 'Wobbling Heights' for its location right on the main road; as big trucks roared past in the night the whole building shook and resonated in sympathy.

"We lived the most outrageous life in the 15 months we were there. Somewhere between *The Young Ones*, and the Manson Family. The police raided us, hoping to bust us for dope, not that they could find any, people came round and beat us up – it was totally mad! There was a never-ending supply of close personal relationships, mostly with all these sixth form girls from the local comprehensive who'd only known the local boys and public school boys. So us, coming into their midst, and being a punk band from London, were far more exotic. They'd come round in the morning to make us cups of tea. You'd be laying in bed and there'd be all these girls coming round for a surreptitious fag and a cup of tea.

"But eventually only Robert and myself were left, he was working days, and me nights, washing up at a restaurant so that we could eat regularly. The never ending battle against the DHSS and sleep finally defeated us. Despite still getting the occasional gig the band finally disintegrated in 1980 and we were forced to return to London."

It was one of the most important periods in his life, enabling Billy to get away from Barking, and home and the route that fate seemed to be proscribing – a 'good job', marriage, kids, mortgage and so on. For Billy and Wiggy it was similar to University, enabling them to sort themselves out as individuals, learning to stand on their own two feet and live on their own terms. But like the graduate who can find no job on graduation, having trained to be in a rock band there was now no band and no gig.

Wiggy started a video company and Billy ran messages for him, as well as doing odd jobs and some painting and decorating. On his way to Wiggy's every day he kept walking past an Army Careers Information Office.

TROOPER BRAGG

"After about a week, I went in and signed up for nine years . . . I couldn't see any other way of getting out of the situation I was in; stuck living back at my mother's, everything I thought my generation was going to achieve had gone to the wall. This was 1980 and the Cold War was hotting up, and I thought if it's really going to happen, you know, World War Three, I'd rather be on the central German Plain than sitting on my arse in Barking. I convinced myself that the Army was the way to do it.

"There was a much deeper thing as well. I wanted to experience the absolute opposite of everything I'd been doing for the last three years, which had been totally undisciplined, I think I was very attracted to having a short, sharp shock administered – a real kick in the pants. I knew I'd either be totally repelled by it, or it would put everything else I'd done in some sort of perspective. It was either that or prison I think."

Like his father before him, Billy went to Catterick Camp in North East Yorkshire for basic training with the Royal Armoured Corps. "There's two things not to be in the British Army: one's black, the other's Catholic. In our intake there weren't either, so they had to make do with the next best thing – southerners. Me and the other southerners got quite a lot of stick, but

if you can be just a little bit sharper, it's very easy to turn their ribbing back on them. As a result, I twice ended up in the Guard House for being cheeky."

After three months' basic training it's possible to buy yourself out of the army, and alienated by the rampant, deep-rooted bigotry, Billy decided to take this option.

"They were all white Anglo-Saxon Protestants, anti-Catholic, anti-black, anti-Semitic out-and-out bigots. Nothing more than you'd see at Ford's of Dagenham or at school, but it was all so much more gung-ho. Singing anti-Catholic songs coming back from the rifle ranges with the Protestant lads who were going to be in my regiment, made me realise they didn't like anyone who wasn't one of them, and I wasn't one of them; I was a punk rocker who liked black music. But I was great at lobbing grenades.

"It was all summed up in some ways when Bob Marley died. I was totally gutted. Me and another guy spent the whole day shell shocked. But the other guys in the regiment just kept asking why we listened to that nigger music. In the end, we went to the corporal, and asked permission to watch the Granada TV tribute on the telly in his room. I had tears in my eyes, and it made me realise how out of place I was there.

"But when I left they were really annoyed, as I had survived everything they had put us through and done well at it. They had tried to destroy us as individuals and then put us back together in the appropriate manner, and here I was wanting to leave, rejecting their whole way of life. It would have been much easier for them if I'd given up in the first couple of weeks, then I could have been dismissed as a weakling.

"My leaving was a relief to everyone I knew, except my mother who thought that, perhaps, I had finally found a proper job. As I came out I said to myself, 'Right; now I know what I'm going to do. I'm going to go solo.' I felt very positive, as if I'd done EST or something. I felt that in some way I was stronger than the British Army. It had been a real sabbatical, I was fit, and really determined to do what I wanted to do. But it is not something I'd recommend to anyone else."

TRAINS, BOATS AND CARS

On his return to Civvy Street Billy got a job in a local record store that specialised in deletions. This was the perfect response to the army, working surrounded by vinyl . . . what more could a vinyl junkie ask for? Not only were there records in abundance but they were cheap and extraordinarily varied: classical Indian music, Indian film music, all sorts of pop, jazz and classical all turned up at random. What was more the manager of the shop had a Portastudio on which Billy was able to record some demos of his songs.

In the last days of Riff Raff he had written a few songs that he thought were finally sounding like his own, rather than pastiches of various heroes. He always reckoned 'Richard' was the first that passed quality control and survived through to his first solo album. But coming out of the Army inspired a whole load of new songs, which was necessary as he had started to do solo gigs, notably as the all-purpose support act at the Tunnel Club in a pub south of the Blackwall

Trooper Bragg, Catterick Camp, June 1981.

Tunnel, called The Mitre. He got the gigs because he cost nothing, his equipment was minimal, and he would play for as long or as little as the public wanted.

The tapes he recorded on that Portastudio in a tower block in the Commercial Road were sent to every record company in London, from Rough Trade to EMI, and they all turned them down or ignored them. Billy also sent them to a *Melody Maker* feature called Playback, which reviewed demo tapes sent in by young hopefuls, this still being the era of the independent. Journalist Adam Sweeting heard the tape and gave it an encouraging review. Reading this, Jeff Chegwin from Chappell Music contacted Billy, heard the tape and liked it enough to offer him some demo time in their tiny studio in Park Street.

There was one company he had not yet covered, the moribund Charisma records, then on its last legs. When he arrived at their reception, he was asked if he had come to repair Tony Stratton Smith's TV set. Having already been to several record companies he knew the vital thing was to get past reception, so he said that he was the TV repair man. He was shown into the offices where he made the TV set worse but managed to

see Pete Jenner, the head of A&R and general dogsbody, and thrust the tape on to him.

To the surprise of them both he liked it. The problem was that Jenner knew no one else in the company would, and the company was so skint they could not afford to spend any money on recording, or the manufacture and the distribution of their records. Billy and Peter both liked the idea of putting out a cheap album which cost little to produce or promote. It was a good thing they did because there was no alternative: Charisma had no money and Billy had no other offers.

So Jeff Chegwin and Chappells paid for Billy to go into their demo studio for three days, and Billy recorded 'Life's A Riot With Spy Vs Spy' straight to stereo. Barney Bubbles designed the sleeve – with the idea that it would be the first in a series of Utility records. Jeff also offered to put up some money for promotion. Part of the deal was that Billy would have to do some of his own promotion (as much as possible in fact), that he would do any gig that came up, and that no money would be spent. The record took forever to release, having to be virtually smuggled out as neither Charisma

The three chums, Kershaw, Bragg, Wiggy, meet at a shoe shop in Leeds 1983.

player."

Much to everyone's surprise, when Billy's first album was released in November 1983, it climbed to number one in the independent charts. There began a frantic period of live gigs that has rarely stopped since. Billy was never particularly fond of the studio, but loved the challenge and the adrenalin rush of working live. From doing any gig that could be found, supporting anyone, anywhere, as long as he had enough money to get there, somewhere to sleep and enough for a meal, people started wanting him to play all over the place.

Originally Billy just got on a train with his guitar and his amp and off he went. "The whole Billy Bragg thing was built on hit and run gigs, supporting everyone, going everywhere. I find the studio a bit boring, being so precise. The cut and thrust of a live performance is what I prefer."

It was all becoming a bit more serious, so he joined up with Andy Kershaw as his driving companion, roadie, publicist and soul mate. Andy had originally picked Billy's album out of the reject bin at Radio Aire in Leeds, where he was the late night 'alternative' DJ. He started playing his record and helped get a couple of gigs together in the Leeds area.

Ultimately the curse of Bragg fell on him too, and he got fired. So obviously he had to become part of the team. Their trips around Britain, and later Europe, became legendary. They argued, insulted and raved at, and with, each other the

nor Phonogram really wanted anything to do with it. When it did come out there were a couple of good reviews, but more importantly John Peel and Janice Long at the BBC, and Andy Kershaw at Radio Aire in Leeds, all noticed it and gave the record night time play.

"Just when it was starting to get a little bit interesting, the pressing ran out and they wouldn't re-press it. Then Jenner got fired, and everything went to the wall. As he'd been the nearest I'd had to professional advice I asked Pete to manage me. As he had nothing else to do he agreed. But once again we had no record company, and despite the few bits of media interest we could not get another record company interested.

"Fortunately, Andy MacDonald stepped in, wanting to put it out on his label Go! Discs! He'd worked for Stiff as a press officer, and he'd just set up on his own in Shepherds Bush. Whenever we played, Andy would turn up, so me and Pete decided that because of his enthusiasm he should at least be given a shot; he's a real music enthusiast, and anyway no one else wanted to know."

As it was only a one-off deal with Charisma I could sign with Go! Discs! but Andy wanted 'Life's A Riot' as well. He asked Charisma for the album.

"'No way', they said, 'he's a Charisma artist, and we think he'll go a long way.' 'All right,' said Andy, 'I'll give you £1500.' They said 'OK', just like that. So I was transferred, just like a football

Kershaw and the battle-wagon.

14

length and breadth of Britain, and a bit more, turning each other on to their varying and different tastes in music. Peter Jenner's old black Volvo estate became a regular feature on the motorways of Europe. For both Andy and Billy these trips were quite an educational experience, much more than just a means of getting from one place to another.

This epic period of crazed activity led up to an appearance on the BBC TV show *Whistle Test*, where Andy formed an instant rapport with the producer while hanging around waiting to go on. In no time he was auditioning for, and being hired as, the new presenter of the show, and getting a BBC Radio 1 show as well. At the same time Billy got his first invitation to visit America and appear at the New Music Seminar in New York.

It did not take long to see that the last thing anyone wanted in the seminar was any new music. So Billy got the ridiculous 'portastack' together, which meant that he could walk around this convention/market place playing his electric guitar and singing, albeit not very well as the weight of the stack made it hard to breathe. The arrival of live music in this fashion caused a sensation, and it took a long time to live it down.

However, it worked, people noticed him and his career in the States was launched. His shows on the roof of the Danceteria with the Empire State Building, swathed in storm clouds and lit by floodlights, as a backdrop, were probably the most spectacular location gigs he has ever done.

After these shows he was invited by Echo And The Bunnymen to open for them on a tour of the US and Canada. This was an unbelievable break, so Billy asked Wiggy to come with him to keep him company, play guitar with him, keep his guitars in tune and to replace the constantly breaking strings – a continuing manifestation of his punk heritage. As no one knew Billy was coming, there was no record available, and as the band just put Billy and Wiggy on their bus, there was remarkably little pressure. They had a chance to get a feel for America, especially its size, and to see many North American towns.

"In my Mum's back room, me and Wiggy used to sit and dream about going to America, so it wouldn't have been the same without him. It meant a lot that he came with me on that tour. The dates ended in Los Angeles, and much to our surprise we found that Santa Monica Boulevard is the end of Route 66. We rented a car and drove right down the Boulevard, which ends at a beach on the Pacific. It was getting twilight as we walked down the beach, and I was getting quite emotional, because we'd actually done what we'd promised ourselves all those years ago at school. We had toured America, coast to coast, as musicians. We then got severely emotional and went and got drunk.

THE UGLY AWAKENING

"In 1982 I'd been in the Army, and out for nine months when the Falklands War happened. At the start I thought it was really out of order going in there, though it was terrible that the Argentinians had one of the worst records for human rights in Latin America. Then when I saw what happened next – all the flag waving and the Task Force, I was appalled – particularly remembering how unpopular Thatcher had been beforehand. When they sank the Belgrano I realised that she was determined to have a shooting war, and couldn't understand why, until it dawned on me that if she won – wrapped herself up in the Union Jack and went through the whole Churchill thing, she'd get another term, and that would upset the Labour/Conservative consensus. The Falklands War prompted my first political thoughts. Even after the '83 election, when she was voted in again, I didn't become a Socialist.

"Margaret Thatcher made me a Socialist. I had all these anti-nuclear, anti-racist, broadly based humanitarian ideals, and found that the ideology that represented some of them was a form of Socialism, so I tried to find out more about it. The great catalyst was really the Miners' Strike. It brought it together for my generation – *this was the struggle*. There were bands like The Redskins, The Style Council, and many others, all writing political songs – but we were writing theoretically. What happened when we got stuck in? No ideology could answer everything, I realised, and there were no absolute answers. It's about applying the ideology of equality – Socialism – to economics."

During this time, Michael Foot lost the election as leader of the Labour Party and Neil Kinnock became leader of the party; Margaret Thatcher was re-elected for a second term.

"The politicising thing for me was that she was going to start changing all the things I'd grown up with and taken for granted, like the Welfare State. It was time to come out and say: this is out of order, and totally wrong. I'd done fund-raisers before – the Campaign for Nuclear Disarmament, and the National Union of Students – but nothing party political. So when the Miners' Strike happened, in March 1984, it was exactly the time I was starting to get my thoughts together with politics; helped by wandering round and picking up booklets at those gigs I did for the GLC (the Greater London Council, the Labour controlled local government body which controlled London and was later abolished by the Thatcher administration), where they had political stalls of different orientations.

"There was one benefit I drove up to in Sunderland for a pit at Wearmouth, and the secretary of the Women's Support Group came to make a speech. She couldn't stand the noise while the support group was on, so she sat with us

in the dressing room. Very calmly, she explained what had been happening since the strike; how her husband and sons, who'd never been in trouble, had been put away or were on remand. How she'd never made a speech, and now had to make them every night. Now she was confronted by coppers everywhere she went, although she'd never been in trouble with the law before. Every morning that she woke up, there'd be five hundred coppers at the pit; they were making her little village into a police state.

"What really shocked me wasn't the North-South divide – I was used to that, even from my experience with the difference between East and West London – but seeing the tactics of Northern Ireland being used to break the Miners' Strike. They forced the miners to strike – none of it was chance. It was a deliberate Tory policy, like the Falklands War.

"That was my political education. We'd never talked about it at home; my father never told my mother how he voted, because he didn't want to influence her."

Neil Kinnock, Billy and Svengali: House of Commons.

When Billy returned from the States the gigs for the miners and the GLC continued, while in between he found time to take 10 days off to record his second album, 'Brewing Up With Billy Bragg'.

This had more explicitly political tracks on it than the first album, but the promotional tour in the UK emphasised his interest in country music and the bizarre, when he teamed up with the Hank Wangford Band and The Frank Chickens for his first major headlining tour. In between, the political gigs went on and the process of politicisation began to bear fruit.

Around Christmas time, with the Miners' Strike still on, Billy had a set of political songs stimulated by recent events ready to record. They came out early in 1985, and, ironically, as the strike ended in March, the EP 'Between The Wars' reached number 15 in the British singles chart. Combined with the songs 'Which Side Are You On', 'The World Turned Upside Down' and 'It Says Here' this EP marked Billy's arrival as a major political song writer and performer.

REVOLUTIONARY TRAVELS

It was while he was doing a gig in Edinburgh during the 1985 Festival with the great Scottish communist singer Dick Gaughan that Billy was approached by a Scottish university lecturer, living in East Berlin, who asked him if he would like to play there.

"I was invited to the 16th Political Song Festival in February 1986, where I was to appear alongside Pete Seeger and singers from all over the Socialist world. During discussions there we said we weren't overly pro the Warsaw Pact, and we had strong differences of opinion with them over human rights, but they said that was fine.

"The festival was an eye opener and quite unlike anything we had been involved in up to that

The Wall as seen from the West.

time. East Berlin made a big impact on me. It's true that it's grey, but that's only because there's no neon. Where my Socialism and theirs diverges is that I'm an internationalist; the young people in East Berlin did feel caged, and keeping people from travelling abroad just makes them want to leave more. But other than that, all the myths were wrong; it reminded me of Essex in the early sixties, lots of concrete new towns. The Alexanderplatz is all new, it was flattened by the RAF, though they're still doing up old museums; obviously you've got to build up the houses and factories first.

"The big talking point of the Festival was Gorbachev, who had just become General Secretary, and the 27th Congress of the Communist Party of the Soviet Union was scheduled to take place in a couple of weeks. The air was crackling with anticipation of this event. We asked for, and obtained, a 'friendship meeting' with the group from the Soviet Union. These are strange affairs, a ritualistic encounter where friendship, desire for peace and other unobjectionable sentiments are expressed while flags, records and other minor gifts are exchanged, under the watchful eye of a commissar."

Billy and Peter also met with some Finns, with strong connections with their own Communist Party, who also had their own political song festival.

"They invited us to their festival in June, and

we agreed providing they could get us to do a show in Leningrad. They arranged this and after we had done their shows, they put us on a train from Helsinki to Leningrad's Finland Station, the same route Lenin took when he returned to Russia in 1917. The actual train that he arrived in is still there in the station on display – a shrine – and that was our first contact with the Soviet Union.

"In the Soviet Union the main rock group action is in Leningrad; it's still the window to the West. It's an incredibly beautiful city. The excitement of just being there was like going to America for the first time. There's a tourist element in it. But over and above that there was something much more exciting than America, that would make you talk to your host all evening. I'd leap out of bed in the morning just to experience more of walking the streets, eating in little restaurants. In the Nevsky Prospect there's a big shopping precinct that used to be an old market called the Goviny Dvor, which now has new shops. I learnt more about Russia there than I ever did in school; you learn the alternative history of Europe, like the British Fleet landing in 1919 in Leningrad, the French and the Americans landing further up the coast, the Poles invading from the South. Me and Jenner, who's one of the best educated people I know, kept on getting surprises."

"In Leningrad, writer Art Troitsky pointed out five bullet holes in the Cathedral and said, 'The Nazis did this.' I said, 'Don't worry, Art – you should see what the Red Army did to East Berlin. Now you're quits.'

Shortly after getting back from this trip where Billy met many of the best young musicians, and did a strange show in the lecture theatre of the Komsomol (the youth wing of the Communist Party), he was invited to go to Kiev to attend The Festival Of The Song In The Struggle For Peace – a snappy title if ever there was one. This entailed going to Kiev in the middle of a German tour. He flew to Moscow, took the train to Kiev, and once there did a couple of bizarre gigs, and a huge propaganda TV spectacular, which culminated in 632 people on stage all attempting to sing the Internationale in Ukrainian.

After this he had to get back to Germany, and this meant going by plane at 6.00am from Kiev airport to Moscow. The airport was an hour out of Kiev across the Dnieper, which was wider than the Mississippi, and past the check points checking vehicles for contamination from the Chernobyl misadventure six months earlier.

There followed an unforgettably frightening two-hour flight to Moscow, which the captain seemed to find as disturbing as Billy, and gave Billy a firm commitment not to travel on Aeroflot internal flights. After being met at the airport, one of Moscow's six huge airports, the party was taken to the Komsomol building for a friendship meeting, given a whirlwind tour round the city including Red Square and the GUM department store for a badge consumption opportunity. Then off to another airport for a flight to East Berlin, where the party arrived at an hour earlier than they left Moscow, due to the three-hour time difference. There Billy met some of his old friends from Berlin, before crossing the border into West Germany to a midnight show in the fabulous Loft Club. This 24 hours has entered into Bragg mythology as 'The Longest Day', a day of truly epic length, spanning an enormous divide of distance and culture.

In 1987 Billy was invited to Nicaragua by the poet, Catholic priest and Minister of Culture, Ernesto Cardenal for their International Book Fair. This was his first visit to the Third World, a chance to see 'A Market' and experience tropical rain storms. He stayed at the Hotel Las Mercedes,

At a physical rehabilitation centre for those injured, civilian and military, in the war against the Contras.

built by the government to compete with the American-owned International Hotel where Howard Hughes lived for part of his life. It is now a haunt of CIA operatives.

"I hadn't realised the devastation created by a combination of nature – the 1972 earthquake which killed 20,000 people and levelled all of downtown Managua – and of corrupt politicians. The former dictator Anastasio Samoza Jnr. had leeched all the foreign aid out of the country before it got to the people. His personal fortune had increased from £600 million to £1,600 million – the same sum that the Sandinistas inherited as foreign debt when they won the revolution in 1979.

"My invitation came through work in England for the Nicaragua Solidarity Committee, and I found myself doing gigs in Managua at the Sandinista Cultural Workers Union and the Cinema Altimeria where I opened for the great Nicaraguan songwriter Luis Enrique Mieja Godoy. But the highlight of the Book Festival was a four-hour Meet The People session in which the 300 delegates could question members of the Sandinista Government, including Miguel d'Escoto, the Foreign Minister, Sergio Ramirez, the Vice Presi-

The international search for silly hats continues – Nicaragua 1986.

dent, and Daniel Ortega, the President of Nicaragua. The fact that these people were open to answering questions from the floor impressed upon me how far this experiment in social democracy was progressing. Can you imagine a Labour government laying themselves open like that?

"Perhaps it was only the flight home, cruising over the Northern Honduras, where the Man From Del Monte reigns supreme over the seemingly infinite pineapple and banana plantations, that I realised the score. The US government wants to snuff out the Nicaraguan Revolution because if the people of Honduras, El Salvador and Guatemala follow the Sandinistas' lead, the interests of the American United Fruit Company and their successors will be toppled. Nicaragua has posed the first major challenge to the 1823 Monroe doctrine, when the superpowers carved up the world, and Europeans pulled out of South and Central America, leaving it for the North Americans to control, in exchange for the US leaving Europe a free hand elsewhere.

"It's no picnic in Nicaragua. People still feel the rationing, but there's a war on, it's a siege economy. With all the poverty, there's an immense determination to fight for what they have. The mood was that everyone was waiting to see

whether Reagan was going to invade, it was just a couple of weeks before the Contragate scandal – smuggling drugs in exchange for arms – broke. One 'camposino' at La Dalia in the north told me, 'Before the revolution I had nothing. Now I have this little piece of land. Whoever comes out of the hills to take it from me, I will defend it. And the way I feel about the value of my death for this little piece of land, and the way a young US marine feels about dying for it, are two very different things'."

MEANWHILE IN BLIGHTY

After the Miners' Strike, Billy took part in the Labour Party's Jobs and Industry campaign, specifically for Jobs For Youth. It was a dry run for Red Wedge, with local politicians coming to gigs to talk to the audience, and day events about local political issues.

Red Wedge evolved over a couple of months.

"The next election in 1987 was big in our minds – we all felt it was a real crunch election. What was the Party going to do about young people in the Election, after the Miners' Strike and the abolition of the GLC? Together with sympathetic activists we had a meeting with Neil Kinnock, and said that if the whole Party from the top down didn't want to back us, we'd do it anyway.

"It was never our intention to tell young people to vote Labour, just to use their vote. Labour Party press and publicity people got totally freaked that we wanted to use the word 'Red'; they thought it would make people think the musicians involved were all pinkos. I said, 'We are pinkos – and they'll call us communists anyway, so let's be proud of our convictions and go with it.'

"It was a very eclectic group of people like Hanif Kureish, Neil Spencer, Paul Weller, and Robert Elms, who flitted off quite quickly. The other musicians involved included Lloyd Cole, Frank Chickens, Hank Wangford, Rhoda Dakar, Junior Giscombe and Sarah Jane Morris. The people from Militant came to us to see if we were approachable, which we weren't, 'cos we had no committees to be taken over. The right wing of the Party got fed up with us 'cos we wouldn't tow

Above: Scenic beauty in Nicaragua.

the Party line.

"But the Leader's office was always very good to us, and supported whatever we wanted to do, even if they disagreed with us. It was very important to us that when we produced our leaflet for the election, Kinnock endorsed it in the front; not that he agreed with everything in it, but he thought it was a good forward looking document."

There was a launch for Red Wedge at the House of Commons. "God, that was strange! A lot of unlikely people were there – members of Blue Rondo à la Turk, Peter York . . . it was very strange. The first tour was January 1986, and it was one of the best tours I've ever been on. Me, the Communards, Junior Giscombe, Lorna Gee, The Style Council. Our guests would stay for two or three nights – like one night, a couple of the guys from Madness came, and the next night there were five!

"By the end of the tour, we had Madness, The Smiths, Lloyd Cole and The Commotions . . . the feeling was very good, very positive. There was criticism from all quarters, but you can't run a political idea up the flagpole without getting disagreement . . . I don't think you can afford to take it personally. You can't be right all the time if you're dealing with something like democratic socialism – it's not a constant. I'm more at home with doubters, the people who say – sod it, at least we'll have a go. The alternative is doing nothing, and I'm not prepared to do that."

Red Wedge became a touchstone at the time. "Everyone was asked what they thought of Red Wedge. There's a lot of pressure right now to stamp out anything that doesn't agree with the Government's point of view, whether it's in the Universities, in the cinema, and particularly in television. Political advertising has been stamped on – unless it's pro-Capitalist."

Obviously, losing the Election was an incredi-ble disappointment to Red Wedge. "But you carry on; you don't just give up. Since then, there's been a continuing attack on fundamental human rights; the right wing revolution goes on apace, like the dismantling of the health and education services, the poll tax, Clause 28 . . . the Tories have obviously decided they're the natural party of government. They have so many mouth-pieces in the country – I want to be part of the fight back. Red Wedge gave me the opportunity to put my art, my pop, together with politics and action. Otherwise I couldn't have done it."

The Labour Party is now using the Red Wedge document produced at the Election as the basis for their Youth Policy. They didn't have one before. Now they've got the first Youth Spokes-man on the Front Bench, something we have been campaigning for from the start. What they really need is a Ministry for Youth and Culture.

"We think that the future of Socialism isn't in the work place any more – it's in the communi-ties, so that's where we're going. A lot of workshops, co-operatives, and self-help groups for young unemployed people. There's a lot of lip service paid to the idea of 'youth'; it's a very broad thing. But they are the most exploited people. The Youth Training Scheme is exploita-tion. The pressure on young people now is to conform, to go into stupid schemes to cut the dole figures and undermine wages for the adult market."

The first album, 'Life's A Riot', had been the primal scream of Billy Bragg; 25 years in the making, three days in the recording. It's all about the DIY philosophy which he inherited from punk, and his years on the road. "Then, 'Brewing Up' was – where do we go from here? It was the first LP to carry anything political, though 'To Have And Have Not' on the first album was personally political, which I would still say is the most effective way of doing it."

Billy's 'Talking To The Taxman About Poetry' was released in 1986. The title was prompted by a poem by Vladimir Mayakovsky, in which he attempted to justify to the tax-man that the job of a poet was just a straightforward job, the same as anything else, like labouring, and didn't need special dispensation. The poem summed up much of Billy's feelings about why he became a musician.

In May of 1988, while their Primary Elections were taking place, Billy toured the USA again. His aim was to encourage young Americans to become involved in their elections, no matter how inadequate it may sometimes seem to them. While over there he hooked up with the Democratic Socialists of America and various Central American support groups. Simultaneously a live EP was issued in the States which was followed by Billy's fourth LP 'Workers' Playtime'.

The New Musical Express writer Roy Carr had been asking Billy to take part in a re-recording of The Beatles' 'Sergeant Pepper' since 1987. He chose 'She's Leaving Home', because firstly, he thought he'd be able to play it, and secondly, he thought it was the song that pertained most to the cause of the charity the record's proceeds would benefit, Childline, which provides a free telephone advice line for children who are the victims of physical or sexual abuse.

"It got to 1988, and I hadn't heard anything about it, till Pete rang me up in the studio and said, 'NME need that song. They've put off Terence Trent D'Arby so that you can do it.' My keyboards player, Cara, sang, played piano, and both recorder parts; all I had to do was sing, so we split the credit. I never thought it would even come out.

"It really took off when Esther Rantzen said on the TV that it was her favourite track, and we recorded it live for her in the same film studio in which they'd done 'The Cruel Sea'. It got such a reaction that they made it a single with Wet, Wet, Wet on the other side, and it went to number one; I was as shocked as everybody else."

AND FINALLY

Throughout this period, and right through to the present, which has already seen four trips to the Soviet Union, eight trips to the USA and Canada, trips to most of the West European countries, several of the Eastern European countries, two trips to Japan and visits to Australia and New Zealand, Billy's experiences have been a continuing education. This has been both a personal, professional and a musical journey of never ending surprises, both good and bad. It has been an enjoyment and a torture, a pleasure and a pain. But of all those trips one stands out above them all, those hats . . . those Foolish Finns . . . those Midnights in Moscow . . .

BILLY BRAGG

CHRIS SALEWICZ/ADRIAN BOOT

The wind that whips off the frozen Moskva river and up to the broad steps of the Hotel Ukraine cuts through your thermal underwear like a Cossack's sabre. It is bone-chillingly cold, as it invariably is in Moscow in late November at one in the morning.

On the steps of the 30-storey, showcase hotel, a rather curious scenario is being enacted. Billy Bragg, his manager Peter Jenner, his guitarist blood-brother **Wiggy**, and a good dozen Soviet companions have disgorged from an Intourist coach that has brought them from the Olympic Village on the outskirts of Moscow. There, Billy Bragg has that evening played the last of several shows, each time before an audience of 6,000, in the weight-lifting hall constructed for the 1980 Olympics.

During the coach journey to the Hotel Ukraine a certain amount of vodka has been consumed by the assembled party. But when they attempt to enter the hotel, the Soviet citizens amongst them are turned back by the pair of night porters. In particular, these night porters, who have not responded well to being compared to **Josef Stalin**, have expressed concern about the

Wiggy ★ Billy's lifelong best friend and co-conspirator. Totally committed to life on the road. Much more of a rock star than Billy. Said of the Soviet Union: "We go there because we have a warped sense of humour."

presence of a Soviet female, in her early twenties.

The concern they have expressed has not been popular with the assembled throng. Their reaction has been noticeably vociferous. From doors tucked away in the rear of the vast hallway of the Hotel Ukraine have appeared a trio of men wearing tracksuits; each of these men is short, exceedingly wiry, and pockmarked; they also look as if they are trained to kill with a single finger-thrust. As, in some perverse gesture whose origins are uncertain, the entire Bragg party and its camp-followers opt to stand outside the hotel on the snowy steps, so this trio of human lethal weapons also step outside, and hover, meaningfully, in the shadows of the arch of the revolving doors.

By now several carloads of uniformed constabulary have also arrived on the scene. And Billy Bragg is involved, with the aid of a translator, in a mild verbal fracas with one of Moscow's finest, a man of around his own age, on whose melancholy, drooping moustache ice is already forming.

The policeman asks for the girl's passbook. When she takes it out of her pocket Billy Bragg snatches it from her and stuffs it away inside his MA1 flying jacket. "If you want it," he says to the cop, "you'll have to arrest me." And he proffers his outstretched wrists, as if awaiting handcuffs being applied.

The policeman's expression is grave. He turns away and glances at the several patrol-cars parked at the base of the steps, as though seeking inspiration. Then he again addresses Bragg. "If you are a good *socialist*," he says, "you will give me the passbook."

Bragg is nonplussed; and makes the point that it is because he *is* a good socialist that he is *not* handing it over.

The situation is rather precarious. Clearly it has escalated almost out of control. Steps, it is evident, are required to bring it down to reality. Peter Jenner, previously as actively provocative as anyone present, suddenly, with managerial sleight-of-hand, pulls a compromise out of the bag: Billy will hand over the passbook, if the policeman guarantees that he will only check it and then hand it back to the girl who will be free to leave unhindered.

Everyone, including the cop, breathes a sigh of relief at this opportunity to climb down without any loss of face. Perfunctorily he glances at the passbook, and then, unsmilingly, shakes hands with Billy Bragg. And, with a pair of companions, wanders off into the night, drawing heavily on a cigarette he has immediately lit.

Stalin ★ *Famous international mass murderer, becoming less and less popular. Previously very trendy with lefties. Stock currently very low – suffering badly in the polls, and the Poles suffered from him. Had brief respite during World War II. His name has given rise to the word 'Stalinism', which is not to be used in polite society. Tallinn was not named after Stalin. When Bragg first went to the Soviet Union he didn't dare mention the name of Stalin: now this is quite acceptable, providing it is used in a pejorative manner. Stalin was very famous for giving new meaning to the great Russian tradition of gulags, which has nothing to do with Hungarian food. A current topic of debate is whether he killed more people than Hitler. A tricky aspect is (a) that Stalin was Lenin's mate, and (b) in a manner of speaking he was also Hitler's mate. We could never have such a good Cold War without Stalin – he was a terrific help in this. He had a very good moustache, and a neat line in*

25

heroic poses. A genuine peasant, he was Georgian, not Russian.

Socialist ★ A word about which one argues a lot. See Karl Marx, etc.

The Billy Bragg party, without their Soviet guests, re-enters the Hotel Ukraine. And one reflects that had this incident occurred in Manhattan or Munich or Manchester, Billy Bragg's suggestion that he be arrested would unquestionably have been taken up; and one wonders whether the entire scenario was not akin to a sensitive, poetic rock 'n' roll star's version of throwing a TV set out of a bedroom window.

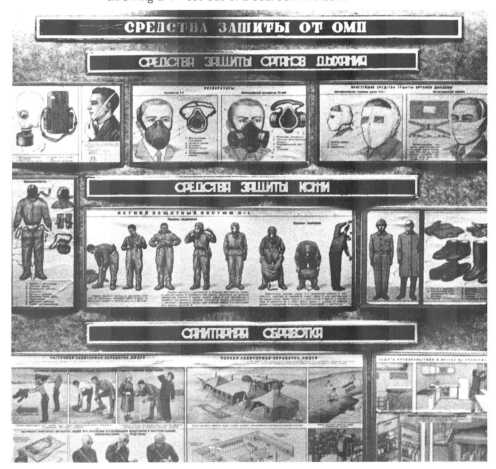

As we leave Helsinki at 10 on a Saturday morning on our way to the Soviet Union, the light in the Finnish capital is dull-grey. It is to remain like that for much of our trip.

We approach the Soviet Union through one of its several back-doors, on a Russian floating casino that ferries Finns from Helsinki to Tallinn, the capital of the Baltic state of Estonia. Though it is a distance of only 40 miles, the boat journey takes six hours. The reason it takes so long is because the boat travels deliberately slowly: the longer it takes, the more **hard currency** may be earned for the Soviet Union from the Finns, a race of people who often seem particularly fearful of any form of ecstasy – and, almost as a consequence, attempt to transcend this fear at every possible opportunity.

By lunchtime we are halfway across the Baltic; half of the **Finns** on board – of a peculiarly redneck variety about whom we have been warned in Helsinki by their countrymen – are in a state of almost total obliteration. Yet for myself the realpolitik of the situation is cast into some perspective in a conversation with a family of expatriate Estonians who are making the

Hard currency ★ *Proper money, as opposed to socialist money.*

Finns ★ *Not Scandinavians. Related to Estonians. Finland is the country over which missiles would explode if the USA and USSR started throwing them at each other. See Hard currency, for Finland is the only country that can convert roubles, thereby Finland is enormously important to the Soviet economy: they take all their oil from the USSR, and supply a lot of expertise – much Western technology gets into Russia via Finland. The fact that Billy Bragg entered the*

Above: The Aurora – the ship which fired the shot signalling the start of the October Revolution. Now a serious 'sight' in Leningrad.

USSR on this trip via Finland was not coincidental. It is the only Western economy which directly borders onto the Soviet Union, apart from Japan. Historically, Finland was regularly occupied by the Russians. A lot of Finns bitterly dislike the Russians. The Finns are very tough, and have had some very bitter and vicious wars with the USSR. The Finns don't seem to worry too much about the Soviet Union: they are aware of their genuine strengths and genuine weaknesses. Quite a nice place, though there is a bad hay fever situation in the summer.

Great Patriotic War ★ World War II in Russia, which started in June, 1941, when the Germans rather unwisely invaded the Soviet Union. They got to within about ten miles of the outskirts of Moscow. Leningrad was virtually flattened, with immense re-building after the war. Twenty million people – one in 10 of the Soviet population – died as a result. The Germans could have been

journey from Stockholm. They are travelling to Tallinn to see a dying relative. It is their first visit to their homeland since they fled, as children, after World War II – or **The Great Patriotic War**, as we come to discover this is known in the USSR. They are deeply suspicious of what awaits them. Beware, they warn, there are microphones everywhere. But there is also, they mention, near perfect reception in Estonia for Finnish television.

For photographer Adrian Boot and myself, this is our first visit to the Soviet Union. We have no idea what to expect, and could just as easily be going to the moon. About Billy Bragg, however, there is a slight air of superiority: this is his third visit to the USSR. He went to Leningrad on an informal visit; and to a similar event at Kiev, only six months after a small incident had taken place at nearby **Chernobyl**. On that visit, Bragg and Wiggy and manager Peter Jenner, discovered that all the food served in the restaurants was virtually inedible. They had assumed this to be part of the fall-out, so to speak, of the Chernobyl disaster. What they didn't realise was that all food stocks from the Chernobyl area had not been destroyed, but processed, the argument being, a classic example of Russian pragmatism, that this would rid the food of any radiation.

Subsequently, Bragg and Co. discovered that the appalling quality of the restaurant food they encountered was nothing to do with Chernobyl: it was due to the internationally renowned Soviet concept of service . . . suffice to say, the British party's suitcases are heavy with muesli bags, and packets of – a little ideological joke here – Red Zinger herbal tea. Billy Bragg also has with him a very large jar of Marmite, the one vital ingredient for a Soviet tour, for large mounds of slightly stale blackish bread are invariably available. Bragg and Jenner offer one of their customary pieces of cracker-barrel advice to us pair of hacks. "Expect the unexpected," they say.

That visit to Kiev had been a 'quickie' – three days and then off to Berlin to return to their tour. Before their internal flight from Kiev took off for Moscow, where they embarked on another plane for the DDR, Billy Bragg had noted the Aeroflot pilot wandering around the plane, kicking at the tyres. (Recently, he recounted, an Aeroflot pilot and his co-pilot had decided to test their blind landing equipment: before a landing, they had covered the cockpit window with brown paper. Over 80 people were killed.)

This trip is far longer. It will last nearly two weeks. There will be

A popular tourist haunt – the battleship Aurora.

stopped sooner, but a Soviet army waited for four months on the Far Eastern front for an attack by the Japanese which never came: when this army moved to the west, backed up by the arrival of another grim Soviet winter, the tide turned. There is a paradox here: Stalin destroyed the leadership of the Soviet army by executing most of the Officer Corps, but mobilised and focused the USSR sufficiently to inflict defeat on the Nazis.

Chernobyl ★ *A vital catalyst: it seemed to reawaken the dormant but great sense of spirituality within the Soviet Union. Also important for the West, (a) because it showed how open was Gorbachev's USSR, and (b) because it was clear evidence of the potential nightmare of nuclear power plants – perhaps one of the most crucial lessons for the Twentieth Century. Important for the British pro-nuclear lobby, because they can now blame all the radiation around Sellafield on Chernobyl.*

Soviet Peace Committee ★ *A semi-official group. Since the earliest days of the Bolsheviks the Soviets have used the notion of the peace offensive. One of the first things they did after the Russian revolution was to withdraw from World War I: 'we've had enough of this' – workers of the world don't need to fight, it's the capitalists who start wars, was part of standard left-wing*

several shows in Tallinn, the Estonian capital, and also in Moscow, with a visit to Leningrad at the end. The dates are being promoted by an organisation known as the **Soviet Peace Committee**. The tour has been set up in Finland, a country which has strong geographical and cultural links with the USSR. And travelling with us is a Finnish pop group called Kadututat. "They're obviously Finland's answer to The Clash," says Bragg. "Every country has their own version of The Clash. And they always get put on the same bill as me." One member of Kadututat is a fisherman, taking unpaid leave from his work. This punk sensibility is of a rather Finnish form, which means that he simply gets drunk a lot. Also with us is a Finnish film crew. They also get drunk a lot. The Finns quickly begin to be referred to by the Bragg party as "These Foolish Finns". By the time our boat docks in Tallinn, most of them are drunk.

Billy Bragg is matter-of-fact about disembarking from the boat. So is his manager, Peter Jenner, a grey-haired man of 45 with a limp and a walking stick that he waves about in a similar patriarchally authoritative way to the manner of Michael Foot and his walking-stick or Michael Manley and his rod of correction. Jenner is a man with a past: he was the first manager of Pink Floyd (he ended his involvement with them when Syd Barrett quit – he was sure Barrett was the real talent), and has also managed Ian Dury, The Clash, Roy Harper, Edgar Broughton, and The Third Ear Band. Currently he also manages Hank Wangford, the C&W singing gynaecologist.

He is considered a rather creative manager. Billy Bragg met him after he bluffed his way into Jenner's office at Charisma Records, where the manager, during one of the occasional lulls in this occupation, had obtained short-lived employment as an A&R man. Bragg had been a fanatical fan of The Clash (the first time I met him was when he supported the Mick Jones-less 'dodgy' Clash at Bristol Colston Hall). And when Bragg met the man who used to paint that group's backdrops and enthused about a former manager of theirs called Pete Jenner, he had to check him out. Accordingly, one day in 1983, he sat in the reception area of Charisma Records attempting to see Jenner. Then a girl stuck her head out of the neighbouring office: "You the bloke who's here to fix the telly?" Bragg nodded, and with one bound was through into the inner sanctum. After they had met, Jenner came to see him play, at the Tunnel in Greenwich. "We must do something together, no matter how insignificant," was his comment after the show. Then Charisma was sold to Virgin Records, and Pete Jenner lost his job. He began to manage Billy Bragg.

As we are disgorged from the boat, Jenner leads the way, along with the Finnish delegation. They are seeking the head of the Peace Committee, who propels them through immigration and customs formalities. Nobody does this for me, however, which is how I come to be stopped for three quarters of an hour because of my copy of *The Waking Giant*, Martin Walker's

cant. But the Peace Committees were one of the first groups to be Gorbacheved and allowed to meet Western peace groups and start talking the untalkable. They are a very key part of Gorbachev's peace offensive: They were one of the first groups to start putting on gigs, outside of the Ministry Of Culture. They are an official part of the structure, but not official in terms of being part of the state cultural apparatus: they can obtain visas and a certain amount of foreign exchange, but they can't make profits. So they are one of the ways of trying to exploit perestroika and glasnost. Not unlike an organisation like CND, if CND had official British government sponsorship. Historically they've always been very good at spotting what the West was doing wrong, but not what the Soviet Union was doing wrong.

Salewicz with offending book.

Gorbachev ★ At an East German song festival in 1986 Bragg and manager Jenner noticed the official Russian group was singing "the thoughts of General Secretary Gorbachev": The thoughts they were singing were based around the slogan "a nuclear-free year 2000". At first Bragg and Jenner laughed at what they thought was yet another corny old Soviet slogan. But then they discovered that the East German and Russian Party members were expectantly looking forward to the XXVII Congress of the CPSU coming up which they knew was going to make a huge difference to the Soviet Union: this was the Congress in 1986 when Gorbachev started coming out with the reality of what was going on in the USSR. There was an enormous excitement about him and about how important a force for change they hoped

Glasnost hasn't reached the official portrait yet.

book on Russia (with an exaggerated wine stain on **Gorbachev's** forehead on the cover illustration of the Soviet leader), and my copy of the *Sunday Times Magazine's* special on the Soviet Union. I'm obliged, I'm eventually told, to present these dissident manuscripts at Customs when I leave the country – and as a consequence, throughout the trip I'm terrified of people borrowing them.

This is all rather as one might expect, and not really all that much different from arriving at Dover by boat. The only difference from what I have been brought up all my life by the media to believe about the inhabitants of the USSR, is that even though these are uniformed officials, they actually appear to be pleasant people. They even smile from time to time. But then, these are Estonians. Perhaps they're not the ones who roast babies on bayonets.

Outside it's cold, though marginally warmer than Finland. The Bragg party, incorporating various already pissed Finns, is lodged on an Intourist bus. There, for half an hour or so, we first experience the seasoned Soviet maxim of 'hurry up and wait'. During this time we meet the official guide with whom we have been presented for our time in Tallinn. An earnest young University student, he is, of course, a paid-up party member. We are certain he reports to the KGB about our ideological soundness. We comment on this in the lift, sailing up to the top of the hotel in which we've had rooms allocated. The lift is rather full. As soon as those dread letters, **K.G.B.**, are voiced, a stony silence falls upon our travelling companions. In future, we always refer to the KGB as the 'Kingston Gas Board' – as in, 'Watch it – Kingston Gas Board situation.'

Travelling with us from Finland, in fact, is someone we suspect of being a Gas Board member. He is part of the film crew, an American, educated in Moscow after his father, an ultra-leftie labour worker, had settled there. Billy christens him 'Joe Blow', and, fairly or unfairly, we become convinced he's spying on us.

The hotel is brand new. It seems to have been built mainly to accommodate the Finns who remain drunk there for the week of their holiday. One of the dangers of travelling in the lifts is that, even at 10 in the morning, they're liable to be full of drunken Finns, many of whom seem to have some sort of alcohol-related problem with personal hygiene. (This is probably to prepare us for the general Soviet problem of personal hygiene,

Joe Blow knows his way around Tallinn with his eyes shut. Finnish film maker Hannu follows behind in his usual worried state.

defined by Billy Bragg as "cabbage breath and BO.")

As he's a famous rock 'n' roll star, Billy Bragg gets a penthouse suite, with its very own record player. There is also, as there is in every room, a colour TV, on which there are four channels with plenty of folk-dancing and classical music. (When we get to Moscow, a paranoid person tells us that the

him to be. In fact, in contrast to the later liberal Western embrace of Gorbie, Soviet citizens have always subsequently expressed disappointment about how little they feel he's so far managed to achieve. Initially he was far more exciting than the West considered him to be. But now he's less exciting, because the reality of his achievements to date is so much less than anticipated. In trying to understand Gorbachev, you realise that the Soviet Union is not nearly as authoritarian and 'single party line' as previously imagined. Certainly Stalin controlled it very tightly, but there have always been different currents of pressure, and different power structures within the Soviet Union. Previously this hasn't come out into the open. With Gorbachev we've been allowed to see the power struggles that have always been going on within the Soviet Union: traditionally you have been allowed to discuss issues until a policy has been made, and then within the Communist party you agree with that policy – unless the policy is to go on talking about it, at which point you continue talking about it. But the idea that everything is totally arbitrary, authoritarian and unresponsive is really very wrong: within each of the Soviet bloc countries there are various power bases, which, like in any other country, the leader must balance and play

off against each other. They are, however, playing to different rules to those in the West and at the end of the day what you can talk about has traditionally been far more restricted, simply because once a decision has been made you can't argue about it. This is where Gorbachev is so different, because he is into dialogue. He is certainly the most important man of the 1980s. If he were an American President he would have been assassinated by now.

KGB ★ *Kingston Gas Board. Is it just an instrument of repression? What it's meant to do is to tell the party what's happening, rather than what's meant to be happening. This is a key role. But in the course of trying to find out what's happening, both nationally and internationally, it becomes very easy to convert it to a position of determining what happens. Equally, however, it is important to realise that the KGB is the body that's been most behind Gorbachev. It was a former boss of the KGB, Andropov, who started the whole thing going: because the KGB realised what a mess the system was in and how corrupt it was, and that something had to give or the whole system was going to collapse. Of*

Former KGB boss, Andropov.

KGB have microphones in the TV sets – though we've already figured out by now that there seems to be something rather dubious about the wires running into the overhead water sprinklers in each room.)

Soon, however, we begin to appreciate that, although the KGB may record millions of conversations a day, there is no possible way they could get it together to listen to them all: we fantasise about vast basements the size of an entire block stacked up with metal canisters of reel-to-reel tapes, growing dustier by the day and the year and the decade.

Through our bedroom windows we can see, in the centre of the town, factory chimneys belching heroic black smoke into the air. With hardly time to be accosted by drunken Finns, we're loaded into an Intourist bus and taken to the Lenin Concert Hall, also known as The Palace of Culture. It is here, on this Saturday night, that Billy Bragg is to perform, with various Soviet acts, as part of a two-day festival organised by the official Estonian Peace Committee.

There's a suggestion that there's an element of scam in this Peace Committee involvement: that because the Soviet Union is still riddled with pre-Gorbachev-style apparatus (**Gosconcert**, the official, inertia-ridden state promoters, for example) alternative routes must be taken to put on non-official shows. Accordingly, a pair of Estonian groovers, Rayne Lang and Reho, a hippy priest look-alike, have sought out an official body behind the façade of which they can bring in Billy Bragg. This is not dissimilar to the days of the Ken Livingstone-controlled Greater London Council who were always accessible to good new arts ideas. Moreover, as Rayne Lang is deputy director of Tallinn's Lenin Concert Hall, he has ample room in which to manoeuvre.

The Lenin Concert Hall, also known as the Palace of Culture, is extremely impressive, on a par with London's Royal Festival Hall. In the backstage area there are walls full of posters offering advice as to what to do in the event of a nuclear attack. Instead of muscle-bound goons, the security is handled by members of the army. This enables Billy Bragg to complete his first badge swap, a precedent for the rest of our stay in the Soviet Union – a Russian military hat insignia in exchange for a cassette of 'Talking To The Taxman About Poetry'. This quote, the title of Bragg's third LP, from the Russian poet **Mayakovsky**, is particularly apt. For joining Bragg on-stage is a local musician and poet, a man of desperate intensity, who models himself on the great Mayakovsky: his group is dressed in a number of revolutionary army

uniforms and civilian costumes. Though this obviously has considerable resonance to the Estonian audience, who applaud heartily, the cynical Westerners can't help but feel that the Mayakovsky musicians, as they become known, look like a variant on several Sgt Peppers.

In front of a backdrop of an enormous peace symbol, Bragg plays a relatively short set, a maximum of 30 minutes. The flow of his act is somewhat interrupted by his insistence that his introductions, as well as an explanation of the theme of each song, are translated into **Estonian**, the language in which all such proceedings take place in Tallinn. Though to my mind, this is by no means Bragg at his best, for he is still finding his way and pace with the audience, the applause he receives is ecstatic.

After the show, we are driven to a local nightclub, on the first floor of a low-rise office complex. The atmosphere is like that at a provincial wedding reception held to celebrate the nuptials of a pair of insurance clerks. That at least is how it seems when we walk in. Within minutes, however, the mood has altered: one that is almost demented sets in after a glass or two of vodka has been imbibed. We drink it with locally produced Pepsi Cola, and it has an effect not dissimilar to that of rocket fuel. "You can see how they got the first **Sputnik** into space so quickly," says Billy Bragg, spooning down mouthfuls of a glass of potato salad; glasses of potato salad are set on every table: we get rather used to glasses of potato salad during our time in the Soviet Union.

course, there is no question that the KGB also has a very sinister side to it: it was founded in 1943 under Stalin as the successor to the OGPU and NKVD and a strong vein from those days still runs through it. They are the secret police, like Britain's MI5, MI6, and Special Branch, but they do more than that. It is probably hard in the Soviet Union to end up working with foreigners unless you have a relationship with the KGB: which doesn't mean you are necessarily a KGB agent – this is because it's a very subtle operation. For many years, however, the KGB were the horror boys.

Gosconcert ★ *For years the only agency allowed to bring in foreign artists and to take Soviet artists abroad. Corrupt in the most archetypal Soviet manner. Totally tied up with*

Above: Assorted musicians at the Tallinn peace concert, including to the right of Billy – Peter Volkonsky, leader of the Mayakovsky group plus two members of Kadutatet.

the Ministry of Culture, and very official, and very boring. "Who are The Pink Floyd?" asked the head of the department responsible for booking pop acts when recently offered that group. An appalling organisation, they epitomise all that is ghastly about the Soviet Union. A close examination of both the KGB and Gosconcert would give a very good understanding of how the Soviet Union works and why it's in the mess it's in.

Vladimir Mayakovsky ★ A truly revolutionary cultural figure, artist, poet, designer and performer who inspires Billy and whose poem 'Talking To The Taxman About Poetry' provided the title for Billy's album. Committed suicide in 1930 after some bad reviews in Pravda.

Peter Volkonsky, the Mayakovsky musician, has a swift conference with each of us. This is rather difficult, as he is already exceedingly drunk, and becoming drunker. He is also exceedingly emotional. Not without reason, one learns. Until **perestroika**, his work had been banned, for the whole of the 1980s. "I am not a dissident, I am an artist," he says, tears pouring down his face, before attempting to lead the conversation into a discussion of the great English writer, James Bond.

The vodka flows freely, even though it is not cheap: three roubles a (full) glass – a rouble is approximately one pound. Many of the local girls begin to look extremely attractive. The various conversations are played out to a soundtrack provided by a house band of a sort you would find playing in a pub in London's West End; its repertoire consists almost entirely of songs Elvis Presley released in his immediate post-Army phase – the band members look as if their army phase was during the Great Patriotic War.

As always, the Finns are indicating a remarkable spiritual oneness with the alcohol on sale. The members of Kadutatet step on to the stage and persuade the band members to loan them their instruments. They launch into a rendition of The Clash's 'White Riot', which, in fact, they had played earlier that evening on-stage when they opened the Peace Committee concert; one member of the group, a fisherman by trade, had been missing: rather

Mayakovsky wonders who has drunk the rider.

Down the A13 trunk road to the East.

unusually, he had got drunk the previous night and missed the boat from Helsinki – he catches up with us the next day and has a few refreshing drinks to celebrate.

Billy Bragg, a man who these days is usually virtually teetotal, observes this. He takes a sip from his vodka and Pepsi. "Come on," he says to photographer Adrian Boot and myself. "You can do the backing vocals on 'Police And Thieves'."

We join him on-stage for a triumphant version of 'Police And Thieves'. "You were truly awful," he says afterwards. Then, backed by Kadutatet, Billy Bragg performs numbers from **The Clash** songbook for at least an hour. 'Career Opportunities', 'I Fought The Law', 'Janie Jones', and – always a huge hit in the USSR, this one – 'I'm So Bored With The USA'. Plus many, many more. Throughout this tour of the USSR, there is much emphasis on the assorted songbook of The Clash. But, to the more than slightly drunk Westerner, sitting in a club on the outskirts of Tallinn in Estonia on a freezing November evening, it does seem somewhat bizarre.

The next morning sees the occasion of an official welcome, or Friendship Meeting, as such events are more precisely known. This is an opportunity for more potato salad. And also for more vodka, though as we all take our first swigs we assume that the innocuous looking blackcurrant coloured concoction we have been handed is fruit juice.

This event takes place in the old town of Tallinn, a beautiful walled picture postcard setting, full of ancient variants on Swiss chalets, with a sprinkling of snow on their roofs, like the setting for a Hammer horror film about Prince Alucard.

Nowadays, of course, it is full of shops that appear to be run by the Soviet equivalent of the British National Trust; they sell rough-hewn sweaters, china, and expensive glassware. By the entrance to the old town, in the spirit of the prevailing perestroika (or 'restructuring') vibe, one notices a selection of stalls selling market produce, notably fruit and vegetables.

The interior of the Quaker-like meeting-house in which the official welcome takes place is immensely ornate – a building full of high ceilinged rooms with gold inlaid architraves. Our hosts turn out to be half a dozen

Estonia ★ Formerly an independent republic and thus very aware of the need for decentralisation from Moscow. Currently pursuing Perestroika to its very limits and possibly pushing their luck. As long as the tanks aren't in the streets of Estonia, perestroika is alive and well. They are relatively westernised, and have one of the highest standards of living in the USSR. They spend a lot of time watching TV from Finland to which they are culturally and linguistically closely related, and this makes them better informed about the West than any other republic in the USSR.

Sputnik ★ On October 4, 1957, the USSR launched its first Sputnik. A terrific PR job. It was simply a hollow ball that contained a radio tracking transmitter which went beep-beep-beep, so it could be followed with a radio telescope. Absolutely freaked the Americans out and led to the first man on the moon. There is also a youth touring operation called Sputnik, and a German language magazine called **Sputnik** which

summarises what has been going on in the Soviet press. It became so interesting that it was banned in East Germany: the final straw was a story about how the German Communist Party, through its general incompetence, had helped Hitler rise to power. The piece was illustrated by two pictures, one of Hitler sitting on a pile of bones, and one of Stalin sitting on an even bigger pile of bones. This was more than the old Stalinists who run East Germany could handle, and they promptly banned the magazine. Sputnik thereby became the first Soviet magazine banned in the DDR.

ПЕРЕСТРОЙКА

Perestroika ★ More important than glasnost. A Russian word which means 're-structuring'. This means completely re-building society: starting from scratch again. The same spirit that was able to re-build the USSR in 1917 and after World War II is now saying let's do it all over again right from the very bottom to the very top.

ГЛАСНОСТЬ

'Glasnost', which essentially means openness, is simply the PR side, the openness of newspapers and media. The most dynamic and widely discussed idea in the Soviet Union since Marxism, with similar global ramifications.

rather elderly, and very respectable looking women. A book on *Peace In Our Time* is presented to Billy Bragg at the end of half an hour of speeches.

This is an encounter with Soviet formalism. The friendship meeting is a bizarre, though very precise ritual, which takes place in all the countries of the Soviet bloc. One is always permitted to make the extremely formal request of asking for a Friendship Meeting. The Bragg posse had first encountered this at the East Berlin song festival, and realised that it was a way to get in touch with the Soviet artists who were present. Accordingly, they asked for one to be organised by their translator, who went scurrying to and fro.

The form of the Friendship Meeting is for the two parties to be ushered into a room, in which they sit on opposite sides of a table, and hand each other gifts – records and T-shirts, in the case of the Bragg party, and books from the Estonian Peace Committee.

Desperate not to offend, everyone in the Bragg party pretends to take it all immensely seriously: Peter Jenner, walking stick in hand, is in his element, looking sombre and severe. Each of the two participating camps ritualistically express their desire for peace and their pleasure about the meeting, and pass compliments about the other's country. No matter how glib such events may sound, they are a very important aspect of Soviet culture. It is hard to discern whether this is a consequence of Communist egalitarianism, or because a lack of old-fashioned deference requires some sort of substitute that can give society some semblance of formal structure.

The assembled party then retires to the room next door. Here they are served more vodka disguised as fruit juice by two girls; these girls in their early twenties are ravishingly beautiful, and in London or New York would undoubtedly have been top models. Another woman then appears, to sing a folk song imploring the world to peace. Then a Russian man plays an extraordinarily boring piano recital. By the time he has finished, the ravishingly beautiful maids have disappeared. The Billy Bragg party leaves.

That afternoon, there is another official visit to be made. Again, this takes place in the old town, in a village hall-like building this time. It is disguised as a meeting of the Tallinn Film Society, and at first involves a vicar-type person introducing a short film about attempts by the State to disrupt the Estonian ecology by ravaging the countryside with open-cast phosphorous mines. With a benign expression on his face, rather like Queen Elizabeth

II would adopt at a similar official function, Billy Bragg watches the film. And then watches the punk group who follow, playing on home-made equipment. This three-piece is fronted by an archetypal Mohican punk. In London he would seem somewhat ideologically suspect. In fact, Billy Bragg and Peter Jenner briefly assess him as being possibly a variant on a typical 'Scally chancer', with an image to suit his 'market'.

When we talk to him afterwards, however, we realise that this fellow – who's bouncing off walls, Sid Vicious-like – is hardly a designer punk: he's the real thing. His name is Villu Tamme, and the song he has sung, set to the tune of a children's nursery rhyme popular in both Estonia and Finland, is called 'Hello, Perestoika'. It is only since perestroika, he tells us, that the local forces of law and order have stopped hassling him. Only two years ago, he and his girlfriend were imprisoned in an isolation hospital for VD sufferers for two months, as a punishment for their unorthodox appearance. He seems bitter about this. But then spits on the floor contemptuously as, in halting English, he concludes his tale.

There is much swapping of badges for the cassettes we have brought with us. Then, somewhat chastened by the punk's story, we return to our hotel to watch some more folk-dancing on the TV.

That evening, before the show begins, Billy Bragg, Adrian Boot, and myself sit in the backstage coffee bar at the Palace of Culture. On a shelf behind the gurgling coffee machine sits a portable colour television set that we glance at from time to time as we chat. Suddenly something rather unexpected catches our attention – a set of commercials, for a brand of chocolate and a make of car. "But they don't have advertisements in the Soviet Union," smiles Bragg ironically. (In fact, the man who has introduced the evening's performances makes commercials for Soviet television. One of the local groovers who had helped organise the event, he later went off to Cannes to exhibit his work at a festival of commercials and won third prize: with 5,000 entries and massive competition from the likes of Saatchi and Saatchi and J. Walter Thompson, Fred from Tallinn waltzes in with one film, gets third prize, and scores a gig making Pierre Cardin's first commercial.)

The next morning, our official guide has arranged for us to be taken round Tallinn on a bus tour. First of all, we are driven to Tallinn's hard currency shop where we buy models of Moskva limousines and try on fur hats: that night we leave for Moscow by train, and although it is snowing in

Villu Tamme
King of the Estonian punks.

The Clash ★ *Punk means a lot in the USSR – it has anti-Party undertones. And The Clash's material was always far more overtly political than that of, say, The Sex Pistols. The Clash and punk were as frightening to the British and American establishment as they were to the Russian. Like all the best rock'n'roll – and The Clash were arguably the best rock 'n' roll group ever – it disturbed the powers-that-be on both sides of the Iron Curtain.*

Cold War ⭐ *Chilly. There is a lot of money in the Cold War, and a lot of power: terrific for selling weapons, and for keeping the lefties down. It made life admirably simple – the Russians were the bad guys, Communism was evil, and we needed all these atomic weapons because otherwise the Russians would bomb us. Justified having McCarthy. Very handy to have a Cold War because you need an enemy to blame everything on – it helps define things. Now the Cold War looks as if it's coming to an end. What will the West do if it doesn't have the Soviet Union as an enemy? How can the British justify MI5 and MI6 otherwise? But will it be allowed to? Because there is so much money to be made from*

Tallinn, we have been told that in Moscow it is as cold as -20 degrees centigrade. The hard currency shop, however, is amazingly hot, even hotter than would be a New York department store in the depths of winter. Such heat, we discover, is a phenomenon of official buildings in the Soviet Union – our hotels in Tallinn, Moscow, and Leningrad are similarly, almost unpleasantly, hot.

We leave the shop, where the Finns have been able to stock up on alcohol, and begin a bus-tour of Tallinn. After we have travelled only a mile or so, we find ourselves in an almost suburban lane; on either side of it, well back from its snowy confines, sit large, wooden, detached houses.

Billy Bragg knows a likely photo location when he sees it. Asking the driver to stop, he and Adrian Boot pile off the bus into the chilly morning air. Our official guide is very put out by this. "Why do you want to take pictures of these buildings: they are old," he points out, with as much understanding as a New York record company executive once expressed when Bragg requested him to drive him around Harlem.

Of course, this explains why, once Boot and Bragg are back on the bus, the guide insists on rigorously controlling our route. When we have been shown the eighth heroic factory, however, we rebel. Although he resolutely refuses to hear our requests to be taken to the docks for a photo session, we insist on being driven to parts of the Old Town we haven't previously seen.

High above Tallinn, Billy Bragg and myself discuss the potential perils of perestroika.

What exactly, I ask him, is the Estonian Peace Committee?

"It's part of the official campaign. Some of it is really, I suppose, propaganda towards the West. I think things have changed a lot in the last year. Since Gorbachev came to power there's been a very definite commitment to sending positive information to the West.

"But, in fact, the Estonian Peace Committee has been going for 26 or 27 years. So it's not something new. But I think that it's great that they've got this peace initiative – I think that's very important. Also, what it does is to give them an official excuse to bring in musicians from abroad. Because the Peace Committee is about International Solidarity, and the young, hip guys, like the ones we've come across, realise the role that music can play in International Solidarity. We have to play those big political shows. But also it gives us a chance to get stuck in to the little clubs like we went to yesterday and to meet people. It also means we can avoid Gosconcert."

Is it interlinked with the Soviet Peace Committee?

"Yes. The whole thing is about Peace Festivals. When we get to Moscow, there'll be an official peace festival, like there was when I went to play in Kiev – that was part of the 'Songs In Search Of Peace Festival', or something like that. What it is is their halfway house between doing things officially and getting an interest going in various bands. I'm sure when UB40 came that they had to play similar shows. Everything But The Girl came as part of the 'World Youth Festival'."

You've now made three visits to the USSR: how has it struck you in comparison to what you'd been told about it before you came here?

"Well, you realise how much of what you're told is simply the bullshit quota. I mean, obviously when you go to America for the first time, it's not exactly like the TV programmes but it is basically similar. But the Soviet Union is so unlike the stuff you get on TV: you know, the way it's sold as a police state. I'm sure there *are* a lot of coppers around, but there are also a lot of coppers around Ladbroke Grove.

"But talking to the ordinary people – that's the most important thing. Talking to ordinary people about what their lives are about. That's what I like doing – looking and seeing with my own eyes and making my own decisions. There are many things in this country that are messed up, you know, that could be a lot better. But certainly it's not the **Cold War** situation we are led to believe."

We seem to have a lot of access to talk to people, don't we?

"But then, why shouldn't we?"

Once back on the bus, Adrian Boot outlines to our guide his plan for a possible photo session. The photo session, however, involves utilising a steam locomotive, of the sort featured in movies such as *Reds*. This, our guide assures us, smiling with irritating condescension, will be impossible. In the workers' paradise of the Soviet Union, modernity is the key-word: such a locomotive will not be found, even if we scour the entire length and breadth of the nation.

We travel another half a mile. Just after we have driven over a level crossing, Adrian Boot gives out a cry of great joy: he has seen just such a railway engine, hidden down some train sidings.

The bus is stopped, and Billy Bragg, Peter Jenner, Adrian Boot, Wiggy,

keeping it going. Of course, one right-wing line, mainly from the older generation, is that the Russians are winning the Cold War, via glasnost and perestroika – which is an evil PR plot to disguise the unchanging reality of Communism. The other right-wing line is that perestroika is recognition that Communism doesn't, and can never, work and that the West has won the Cold War. The Cold War was very good for disseminating a formidable amount of misinformation which is why the Bragg party could go to the Soviet Union and find that most things were totally different from what they'd expected.

МИР ★ Peace

Role reversal – Boot by Bragg.

41

and myself, step across the snowbound railway tracks to where sits, casually emitting blasts of steam, what turns out to be a magnificent specimen of Soviet locomotive, even down to the red star on the front of its boiler. We could hope for no better: if anything, such powerful synchronicity is firm proof that in the Soviet Union, there most certainly is the presence of a God.

Back on the bus, the photo session successfully completed with the spirit of eager train-spotters, our guide does not acknowledge what has occurred: the locomotive does not exist.

But early that evening we encounter a locomotive whose existence is unquestionable. It is the 7.00pm Tallinn to Moscow non-stop sleeper. As we board it, the dull grey sky has already been the colour of night for several hours.

There is great excitement about this 800-mile journey. The artistic history of Russia is filled with adventures that take place on the vast network of railway tracks that bind together this vast continent, Tolstoy's *Anna*

Battleship Potemkin ★
*Many people's impressions of
what the Soviet Union is like,
even today, come from
Eisenstein's film Battleship
Potemkin. It is a grainy,
black-and-white world in
which everyone wears long
grey coats and long pointed
beards, and move in the
staccato way of silent cinema
stars as they trudge through
the snow. But Battleship
Potemkin is a terrific film,
with the Odessa Steps
massacre frequently
replicated in subsequent films,
most recently in Brian De
Palma's 1988 Oscar-winning
The Untouchables, in the
Chicago railway station shoot-
out scene. The events on which*

Karenina, for example. And there is something almost indescribably romantic about Soviet trains.

Our journey to Moscow proves to be no exception. Snow, for example, has formed in thick flurries on the enclosed platforms that link each carriage and to which smokers are exiled. Samovars of delicious Russian black tea are brought to the compartments by the male member of the trio of staff who service our carriage; each carriage has a similar team; there is no unemployment in the Soviet Union, but there is plenty of underemployment – there is some concern that perestroika, and the creation of something akin to a market economy, may alter all this. Mind you, it no doubt requires a number of hands to continually stoke the coal-fired boiler on each carriage that heats the individual central heating systems.

In the spirit of such films as Boris Pasternak's *Dr Zhivago*, we sit huddled together in one compartment and, for many hours, discuss life like men. Principally, the life we discuss, over yogurt and tea, is that of the people of the USSR.

The working references for this historical overview of our visit to

the USSR which lasts deep into the chilly night, are my almost confiscated copy of Martin Walker's *The Waking Giant* , and H.G. Wells' *A Short History Of The World*.

Billy Bragg is very strong on ideologically sound anecdotes that do not form part of the English school system's curriculum. He tells, for example, a story of how working-class revolutionaries in the North of England immediately after October, 1917, were ruthlessly suppressed in a near-massacre along the lines of the **Battleship Potemkin**. He tells about Samantha Smith, a 13-year-old American girl who wrote a letter to the Kremlin and went to visit it, and was then killed in a plane crash. He insists the reason the USSR has taken over control of the **Warsaw Pact** countries of Afghanistan is because of justified paranoia, because Russia has been invaded so many times – even by the West, immediately after the Revolution – and that the country's inhabitants wanted to barricade themselves off from potential attackers. Peter Jenner sums up the discussion: "Is there anyone who does not believe that Solzhenitsyn was used and promoted by the CIA?"

The seriousness of our evening is maintained when the discussion wanders on to the topic of the significance of, first, The Faces, and then early Motown. The mood, as we struggle to attain status by producing ever groovier muesli bars, is not unlike that of The Famous Five Go To Moscow.

As we continue our relentless journey, all we see out of the icy windows are hundreds of miles of flat, snowy pine forests. Obviously moved by the similarity with their homeland, the Finns celebrate in their own compartment by getting blind drunk. At some point, late in the evening, Adrian Boot and myself hold a small summit meeting to discuss our impressions of the Soviet Union so far. Essentially, we feel, everything we have been told all our lives about the Soviet Union is bullshit.

Eventually, in the early hours of the morning, we fall asleep. We are awakened by glass mugs of tea being brought to us by one of our carriage attendants. Outside the windows the view has changed: the terrain remains remorselessly flat; but the pine forests have begun to disappear, to be replaced by mile after mile of dachas (which resemble large garden sheds), belonging to upwardly mobile Muskovites. Every so often, we see frozen lakes, on which sit anglers, fishing through holes in the ice. As we draw closer to Moscow, we make out, more and more frequently, dark, almost satanic industrial complexes, from which black smoke belches.

Eisenstein based his film occurred in 1905 in Leningrad, part of the unsuccessful revolution of that year. Stalin's espousal of Eisenstein was reluctant: it came about after Stalin became aware that the world was perceiving the Soviet Union through Eisenstein's films, and subsequently took him under his wing, though insisting on a certain amount of editorial control. The film that really ran Eisenstein into trouble was Ivan The Terrible, an allegory in which Ivan stood in for Stalin. Part One showed him putting the country together. But by Part Two he was certainly acting rather strangely, and consequently Part Three was never completed.

Warsaw Pact ★ The necessary corollary of NATO.

At nine o'clock in the morning, we pull into Moscow's Leningrad Station. As we disembark, we are attacked by the almost unbelievable cold, a far more intense chill than in Tallinn, a consequence of Moscow's location in the midst of the continental land mass of the Soviet Union. All around the station, there is serious, deep snow, everything you might have ever imagined a Russian winter to be like, hell-on-ice. On the tracks on the other side of the platform to where we have pulled in, there is a train bound for the Arctic Circle, on to which soldiers are piling, snow shoes and skis strapped to their baggage.

Billy discovers why there is no unemployment in the USSR.

Our official guides meet us off the train. Just to simplify matters, they are both named Sasha. Bragg, Jenner, and Wiggy have met them before: they had accompanied them on the trip to Kiev. The smaller, but rather rotund Sasha had played guitar during the train journey to Kiev: henceforth he became known as Guitar Sasha; the leaner, taller Sasha is a huge fan of Ultravox: naturally, he is known as Ultravox Sasha. Guitar Sasha is further identified by his immense happiness that Uriah Heep are due to visit Moscow for two weeks after Billy Bragg returns to the United Kingdom (undeterred by the fact that this decade almost no one in the Western world has cast even a thought in the direction of Uriah Heep, the Soviet audience anticipate the arrival of the, "Very 'Eavy, Very 'Umble" group with unseemly enthusiasm). The Billy Bragg party, who consider themselves to be quite definitively post-1977, find this rather troubling. Uriah Heep ultimately bombed, we are later relieved to hear.

Church and Hotel Rossiya, where the service is as inspired as the architecture.

The Hotel Ukraine: one of 'Stalin's teeth'.

Scattered about Moscow are a series of vast buildings, constructed in the early 1950s on the instructions of Stalin. Built on immensely broad bases, occupying an entire block, they culminate some 30 or so floors up in a set of tall spires. Modern semi-skyscrapers, they have a Gothic, mediaeval look about them, like something from **Eisenstein's Ivan The Terrible**. More than anything, they resemble those turn of the century hotels built in Chicago or Manhattan – the Essex House on Central Park South, for example. Clearly they were intended by Stalin to state that Moscow was equally as macho and phallic as the United States when it came to power-architecture. And these constructions, classic examples of Stalinist architecture, came to be known colloquially as 'Stalin's Teeth'.

Left: Art Troitsky (right) and Guitar Sasha (back) meet the train at Moscow station.

Ivan The Terrible ★ See also under Battleship Potemkin page 44

Boris Grebenschikov ★ The leader of Leningrad's Aquarium. The first Soviet rock musician to record in New York, where he has made an LP for CBS produced by Dave Stewart, and one of the stars of the 1988 New Music seminar. Huge in the Soviet Union, and a great star in a sort of paternal Grateful Dead mould. A warm, charming, genuine, interesting, and very mystic man. He made Billy's first trip to Leningrad unforgettable, and the Moscow concert on this trip so successful.

Boris Grebenschikov.

Zhanna Aguzarova,

It is in one such edifice, the Hotel Ukraine, that the Billy Bragg contingent, incorporating the Foolish Finns, is lodged. The vast, overheated foyer is packed with a clientèle whose internationalism is as apparent in the mix of different skin shades as it is in the variety of tongues. The Billy Bragg party is astonished by the staggering beauty of what we assume to be a party of Japanese women. But here our naïvety is showing: the women are speaking French and are, of course, Vietnamese. In fact, almost all the thousands of hotel rooms in the Hotel Ukraine are occupied by guests from the Communist countries, or countries with strong links with the USSR.

The spirit of hurry up and wait looms powerfully over the Hotel Ukraine. Although we have arrived at the hotel by 9.30 in the morning, it is after midday by the time the last of us has been registered. Initially, we ascribe this to the fact that virtually no businesses in the Soviet Union are computerised: according to Martin Walker, this is also why there are virtually no photocopiers in the country – so that the spread of information can be kept firmly under control.

However, when we glance over the wide mahogany reception desk what is the first object that greets us? Of course: a word processor.

At least this wait has allowed us time to slake our thirst on pineapple and mango juice, and quell our rebelliously rumbling stomachs with black or red caviar and black bread – three roubles a portion in the café at the rear of the entrance foyer. Nearby is the British Trade Delegation. For most of this trip to the USSR our stomachs are in a fairly immense state of turmoil.

That afternoon, the two Sachas accompany us to the official Moscow Peace Committee reception. This is held in an official room in an official building, with official snow outside. As well as Billy Bragg, there is also present one of the acts who will be on the bill with Billy as he plays his four nights of shows. Unfortunately the legendary **Boris Grebenschikov**, of the Leningrad group Aquarium, has not yet arrived in Moscow. But present are the group Bravo, notably their singer Zhanna Aguzarova, a woman of great beauty despite an extreme hooked nose. Her physical attractiveness contrasts sharply with an awkward aura: she is later revealed to be a woman with a most overdeveloped sense of her own stardom. More interesting is the poetess, the witch queen of Georgia who, wearing her other hat of psychic healer, regularly massaged **Brezhnev's** prostate during the latter years of his life. Officials flutter around this woman of an evident **Rasputin**-like influence.

Rather appropriately, one feels, this woman in her early fifties is never without her toy-boy.

This official welcome to Moscow takes the form of a similar, but more sophisticated, mutual back-slapping to that which took place in Tallinn.

After Billy Bragg has taken part in the requisite number of brief radio and press interviews, we are ushered back on to our coach. We don't know where we're going, but there seems to be rather more people accompanying us now.

We wind up on the banks of the frozen Moskva river, in Gorky Park. Instead of discovering faceless corpses, as in the novel, we discover Soviet citizens jogging, the ubiquitous nylon leisure track-suits for once having a practical purpose. And we find the USSR's very first independent recording studio. No one from *Melodia*, the official Soviet record label, has anything to do with this relatively rudimentary set-up, at the rear of a 10,000-seat open-air amphitheatre that in winter is slippery with ice.

This complex is owned and operated by Stas Namin, an important figure on the Soviet rock 'n' roll front with relations in 'high places'. Nasmin is a member of the wheeler-dealer tribe of Soviet Armenians: the phrase 'Armenian Mafia' is heard from time to time, and though the bravely

Brezhnev ★ *Severe problems with and for his son-in-law. All that's dreadful about the Soviet Union. It's potato time! Dead for a very long time before they buried him. Incompetent, corrupt, lazy, inert. His period in power is now referred to as The Period Of Stagnation. Everything simply stopped, apart from corruption, which flourished. Dreadful person. But Soviet rock music did get going under Brezhnev, largely because no one could be bothered to really suppress it but equally no one was able to get it on officially. An era of cynicism and frustration.*

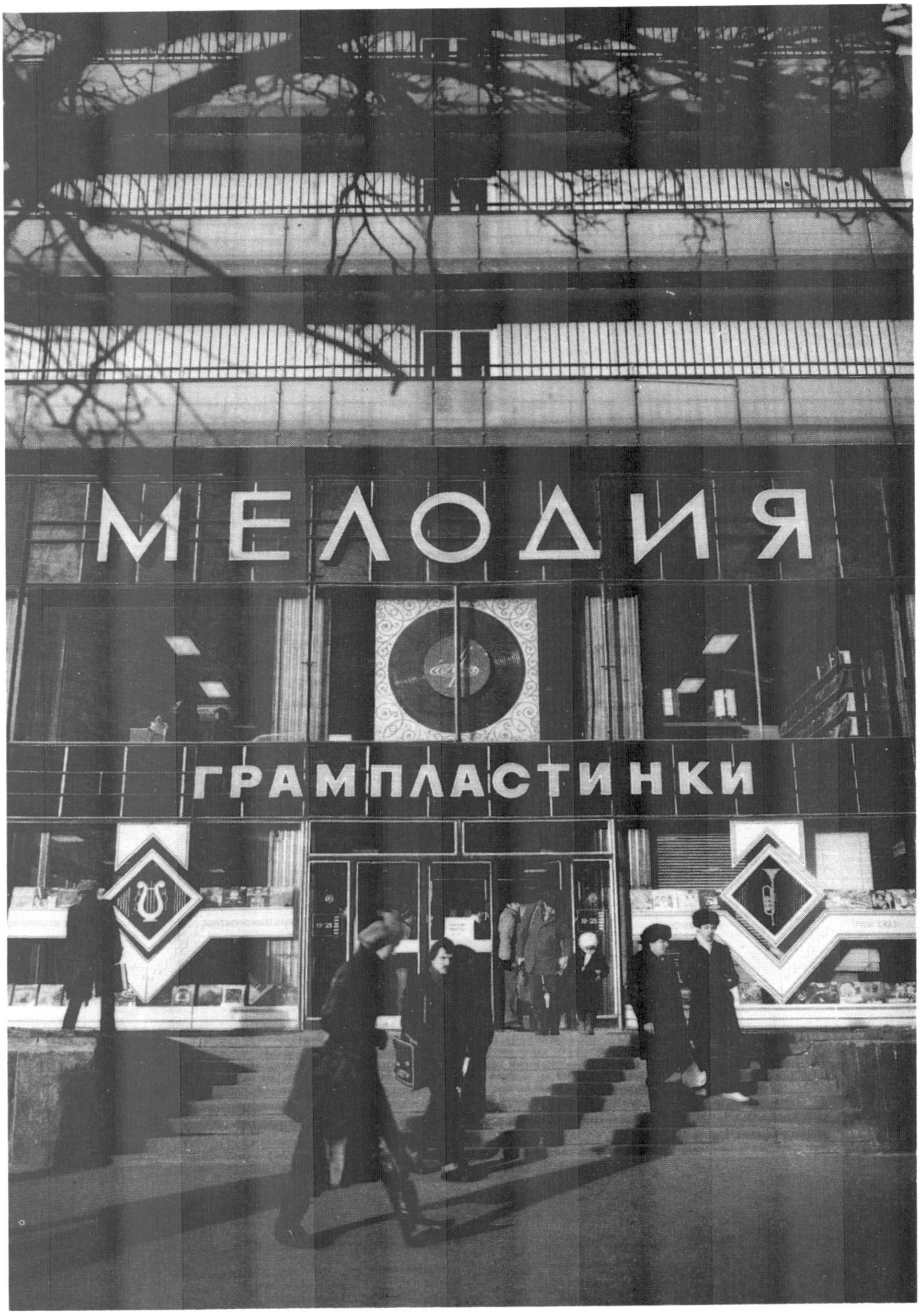
МЕЛОДИЯ
ГРАМПЛАСТИНКИ

pioneering Stas should not be included in such a categorisation, there certainly seems to be disproportionate connections between Soviet Armenians and organised crime.

It is while we are at the recording studio that the Billy Bragg party first pay serious attention to a somewhat sinister figure: a short, slim man, with striking Mongolian features, wearing an **astrakhan** hat and ankle-length black coat with an astrakhan collar. Questions are casually put to him in an endeavour to ascertain his purpose. He claims to be a journalist. Billy Bragg immediately offers to give him an exclusive interview. The offer is regretfully declined; the astrakhan-clad journalist does not have his tape-recorder or notebook with him, he says. A notebook is immediately offered to the fellow. Now his excuse is that he has been unable to do sufficient research. The Billy Bragg party come to only one conclusion: this seems to be a definite Kingston Gas Board situation. We make our excuses and leave him there.

That evening Billy Bragg plays his first concert in Moscow. It is at an *official* music club. This means it is a rather boring business. Since Gorbachev, in an effort to end the chronic alcoholism that plagues so many areas of Soviet life, has declared a state of near-prohibition, alcohol is rarely found in Moscow – as opposed to the more relaxed state of affairs in Tallinn. And it would never have been on sale anyway in this situation: smoking – and everyone in the USSR seems to smoke – is not even allowed.

This official Moscow club also enjoys an immensely inconvenient location, at an area known as 27 kilometres, which of course indicates its distance from the centre of Moscow: there are various zones in Moscow, based on the distance of their radius from Red Square – the 10 kilometre zone, the 20 kilometre zone, and so on . . . It seems appropriate that on the way there Billy Bragg and myself are provided with a serious analysis of Soviet youth problems by a young psychiatrist, a friend of Ultravox Sacha's. This psychiatrist's work involves him dealing solely with 14-18-year-olds with mental health problems, all of whom are incarcerated in the hospital in which he works.

"They don't want to work," he insists. "All they want to do is drink and make love." We try to explain that in the West this was known as The

Rasputin ★ *The first Russian superstar. A monk, who was supposedly mad, though obviously not. Grigori Rasputin was a supposed prophet and healer who was thought to be able to cure the haemophilia of the Czar's children, and thus had great power over the Tsarina Alexandra, believed by many to be the real source of power in the last ruling Russian royal family: Rasputin was suspected of bonking the Tsarina. He allegedly ran Russia, and was essentially part of the great Russian mystic tradition. Very good image but piss poor PR.*

The Mad Monk himself.

Melodia ★ *Spiritually like an English record company before Elvis: about as hip and woefully ignorant about marketing. Melodia has managed to achieve what all the American majors would love to achieve: a total*

monopoly, and an ability to be completely mediocre, and to make nothing but money with any old shit they put out. But Gorbachev has now put some new people in, with a brief to liven things up: they seem now to be showing signs of life and attempting to relate to the Twentieth Century.

Astrakhan ★ *Skin with black curled wool from very young lambs. Very elegant looking. Very bad vibe. But ever so warm.*

Art Troitsky ★ *Please note the 'i'. Soviet media star and ace face. The author of* **Back In The USSR,** *a crucial text. He is Russia's foremost rock commentator and critic and the organiser of the Chernobyl disaster fund concert. In 1984 he was banned from the Soviet official press for suggesting a more liberal attitude towards the Soviet rock movement. Under Mikhail Gorbachev he was reinstated to his former position. Billy's first and best guide through the many contradictions of Soviet life and music.*

Spirit Of 1967, or even of 1977, but to no avail. To cure such untidy thinkers they are given drugs from East Germany, Poland, and the West. The eyes of Billy Bragg and myself meet and, bridling somewhat at this archetypal Soviet response to unorthodox behaviour, we endeavour to engage the psychiatrist in debate about this troubling solution to 'youth problems'. We mutter to each other about the Tallinn punk who'd been imprisoned in the isolation hospital: language problems, unfortunately, prevent further discussion.

The Music Club at kilometre 27 resembles the sort of youth club you might find tucked away on the edge of a council estate in the Midlands – beyond the 10 kilometre radius, most of Moscow resembles the delightful tower block modernity of, say, Basildon. The audience – no more than 200 strong – in this *boite* drinks mango juice or sips coffee and nibbles at ice-cream as a succession of groups play for them. The most spectacular of these sets of musicians, which include an outfit clearly modelled on Motley Crue, is called Last Chance: they are a balalaika group whose songs are based on revolutionary poems of the twenties. Last Chance play plenty of free concerts, particularly in orphanages: we like them a lot as people and as musicians. There is also another, rather punky group called Martin, all of whom live nearby, and their singer, Serge Kuprishov tells me forcefully, "My country is the greatest country in the world." This is a view we hear rather a lot; *Art Troitsky*, the Russian rock critic, views the USSR as a superpower at least on a level with the USA. Largely speaking, notions of nationalism have not yet been transcended in the Soviet Union, another similarity between this superpower and the rival USA. Soviet music fans, according to Art Troitsky, feel a much greater affinity with English music than American: all the same, it's a pity Bob Marley never played there to offer his message of One Love, One World.

It is also slightly confusing for them when Billy Bragg plays a number he recorded with Wiggy while in the group Riff Raff. It is called 'I Wanna Be A Cosmonaut', and celebrates Yuri Gagarin, who sailed around the world in a sputnik, as 'the first punk cosmonaut'. This causes a measure of confusion in the audience. "I thought it was brilliant," Bragg explains to me afterwards. "The Americans had all these soft landings in the sea. But after Gagarin re-entered the earth's atmosphere, he just climbed out of his capsule with a parachute on and floated down to land on the Siberian steppes." What one might call The Left Stuff, I suppose.

Boot gets arty.

The next night is the first show of Billy Bragg's four-night engagement at the Moscow Olympic Village. Again, this is situated some distance from the centre of Moscow. "It looks just like it is off Riverside Drive in Manhattan here, doesn't it," says Bill, as we cross over the Moskva river on our way there.

It is in the weight-lifting hall, in which the stench of sweat still lingers, of the Olympic Village that the concerts are to take place. This edifice is constructed, as is the rest of the Olympic Village, in that fashionable eastern block style of architecture that comprises lumps of concrete stuck together at right angles. In order to maintain the neo-Bauhaus workers' feel the inside of the hall has been left undecorated: the inside of the weight-lifters' hall is determinedly modern and functional almost to a point of pretentiousness.

Art Troitsky, don't forget the 'i'.

Unfortunately, however, the PA is not as it should be. There is, in fact, no bass amp. We now discover that the reason we visited Stas Namin's studio in Gorky Park was to see if they had one we could borrow (they didn't).

Inevitably, the director and producer of the show is called Sasha, Sasha Voronkow. He has also written the script for the show, along with the poetess/prostate masseuse. An unctuous figure, Voronkow's determined efforts to evince a total 'no problem' vibe are beginning to wear thin: the show is due to start in three hours' time. Peter Jenner switches into stadium rock manager mode and, on the stage in front of a good 30 of the crew, loudly berates Sasha Voronkow, who is also known as The Fat Controller, for his incompetence. His ego severely wounded, stage manager Sasha visibly bristles and displays a most unpleasant side of his personality. "You will regret this," he snaps, as sinisterly as he can. Jenner laughs at him: "Fuck off. What are you going to do? Send me to *Siberia*?"

The western contingent, as well as the assembled members of Aquarium, who have never witnessed such a scene in the Soviet Union, are rather impressed with such daring fighting words from Jenner. While we wait for them to sink in we decide to enjoy the set dinner provided for us late each afternoon.

This takes place in an Olympic Village hotel, the Ismailova B (naturally, there's also an Ismailova A, C, and D) some half a dozen blocks away.

Fat Sasha – Perestroika still has a lot more work to do.

Siberia ★ *Very big and a lot of it. A lot of gulags also. Once a lot of Siberian tigers, though not so many now. A lot of good music there now. Being sent to Siberia was worse than being sent to Coventry.*

Aquarium at the Moscow concerts – the spirit of Woodstock is not dead.

Although clearly recently constructed, its modernity is of a rather grim nature. This grimness is characterised by the post-nuclear holocaust half-light that surrounds the building and permeates every atom of its interior, even those areas with an abundance of electric lighting. And this post-Big Bomb feel is maintained by the nutrition placed before us. The style in which it arrives at our table is in accord with that great Soviet tradition of service we already have encountered in such consumer-friendly establishments as Moscow's GUM department store: in other words, the plates of food are whacked down in front of us with a surliness that could only be the consequence of centuries of serfdom.

But as Octavius Caesar said of Enobarbus in Shakespeare's *Anthony And Cleopatra*, it is not the manner but the matter which is so bleedin' offensive. For the fish we are served has a distinctly Chernobyl vibe about it: it is so green it is almost glowing. None of us are greatly fussy about our food. But both Bragg and myself are obliged to look away from our plates in order to prevent ourselves retching. As one, the Bragg party rises from the table and returns to the weight-lifting hall.

Billy and Boris pass the time of day.

Group shot from the Moscow concerts.

Back at the venue, with the first major Moscow show still 90 minutes away, we discover what Billy dubs as "the perestroika coffee-bar" in the foyer of the weight-lifting hall. Here ice-cream and assorted gateaux, and coffee and fruit juice may be obtained. It is a welcome relief from Billy Bragg's dressing-room, which appears to have no heating in it whatsoever, despite more than 10 degrees of frost outside. With its exterior wall comprised entirely of glass, it is formidably cold. The only points to commend the dressing-room are the greaseproof-paper packets of cheese sandwiches and apples which every day are placed there: we do not return to the nearby hotel for any further meals.

At this immediate pre-show stage, a certain controversy is taking place. The concert's management committee has requested that the assembled musicians – Billy Bragg, Aquarium and Bravo – join together at the end of the show on one anthemic number. 'Yellow Submarine' is the song they suggest, which naturally is received with utter derision – though when Bragg realises he could adapt it to, 'We all live in a yellow Polaris submarine', there do seem to be some possibilities. Eventually, after discussions between Billy Bragg and Boris Grebenschikov, the leader of Aquarium, a compromise is reached. The musicians *will* play a final number together, but it will be 'Get Up, Stand Up' by Peter Tosh, who had been shot dead only a month previously.

This 'Yellow Submarine' business turns out to be the poetess/prostate masseuse's idea. She came up with the concept for the show, and it is on her account that the rear of the stage is draped with a cloth painting of a deer being hunted down by a beastly hunter.

The Aquarium collective benefit from a large, warm dressing-room. And inside is an atmosphere not at all dissimilar from that backstage at a similar event at, say, London's Hammersmith Odeon: plenty of quite beautiful, rather coquettish girls are in evidence. But there are certainly no drugs; one member present had recently served four years in a labour camp for possessing one grain of opium.

Aquarium are from Leningrad. We have learned, during our time in the USSR, that Leningrad has a reputation as a city that is more conducive to the arts than Moscow. Moscow has 12-lane highways running through the centre

The plot continues.

A member of Kadutatet.

of the city, jammed with rush-hour Volgas and Moskovitch cars, and massive trucks and trolleybuses, as well as the occasional sleek black Cheika or huge black Zil limousines roaring down the élite centre lanes of the highways.

Certainly Moscow is considered the economic centre of this socialist empire. Leningrad is as, say, San Francisco is to Los Angeles, or Edinburgh to London. Boris Grebenschikov and the rest of his group have come from Leningrad by train, and are intending to remain in Moscow for as short a time as they can. "In Moscow," Grebenschikov makes a complaint that could apply to any capital city in the world, "everyone's having lunch 24 hours a day, making deals. Everyone talks business here all the time. In Leningrad no one talks business."

Art Troitsky, a Moscovite and the leading Soviet commentator on popular culture (his book, *Back In The USSR*, is indispensable), looks visibly miffed when, minutes later in the same dressing-room, I mention this to him. But then again there's a vast difference between the striving Troitsky, fascinated by such notions as post-modernism, and Aquarium, a group that celebrates both traditional and modern music in a beautiful and lyrical way. Mind you, Billy Bragg is somewhat bemused when a couple of members of Aquarium, seeing him handing out tapes he's brought to the USSR, inquire whether he has any Jethro Tull LPs with him.

As a matter of fact, one may well be bemused by plenty that is taking place here, notably the acts being presented each night to an audience of 6,000 people. There are the rock 'n' roll acts that might be expected: Bragg, of course, and Aquarium, and Bravo, and Kadututat, the Finnish Clash. But there is also the psychic poet/prostate masseuse. And a woman dressed up as a duck, one of several characters who dance to a tape of 'Una Paloma Blanca'.

It is Kadututat who draw the short straw and begin the shows. Anyone in the audience of even a moderate punky sensibility is attracted to them. Which means that at least 90 per cent of the audience thoroughly abhor them. Still, as an irritant factor, Kadututat certainly succeed.

Bravo are next. Their Russian brand of rockabilly has proved so popular that their first official LP, on Melodia, has sold over a million copies. (High sales are not unusual in the USSR for popular artists: one female vocalist, Alla Pugachova, has sold over 160 million copies . . .). None of the Bravo musicians, however, has earned over one hundred pounds from this venture; Yevgeny Khavtan, the main songwriter, however, has really cleaned

Live – *Zhanna Aguzarova, Bravo.*

up, with at least £1500 made to put away to that dacha in the north Moscow suburbs. Bravo's stage-set is exciting and visual, although there are some who claim they have been playing it for the last five years. Zhanna, the singer, is also a bit of a pain, with some pop superstar attitudes that disappeared in the United Kingdom – though not in the United States – in the mid-seventies: when Billy Bragg gives her a packet of cigarettes, she moans at not being given a carton; when he hands her a couple of cassettes, she suggests, with no trace of irony, that the next time he's in the Soviet Union he should bring instruments for her instead.

Before Billy Bragg goes on-stage he is visited in his dressing-room by members of a Soviet underground band. They give him a copy of a book and a record by the man they tell him was the Soviet Union's first punk artist – Lenin. "The first Russian rock 'n' roll star? Yes, I'll buy that. He was quite a punk, bit of a star. As you can see, much like Elvis, they put his face up everywhere." They also give him a hammer and sickle badge, which he proudly wears on the thick woollen sweater that the Estonian peace committee had gratefully given him.

Also visiting Billy Bragg in his dressing-room is Leonid Zakharov, the music writer from *Construction News*, the magazine for the union of building-site workers, which has a huge circulation. He is an immense fan of Studio One music, that most esoteric and stirring of reggae music produced by the master, Coxsone Dodd. We find this somewhat amazing as his knowledge of the music goes back to a time when remarkably few white people in Britain even knew about it.

By a nice twist of *Jah!* Billy has with him a recent Studio One Greatest Hits compilation – he gives it to our man from *Construction News*. We also meet a writer with the celebrated Soviet paper, *Tass*. He tells us that he recently contributed to an article on glasnost for *The News On Sunday*. Is it usual, he wonders, for UK papers to pay their contributors? Don't worry, I tell him, I'll sort this out when I get back – they owe me money too. When I return to Britain I find *The News On Sunday* has folded.

Bragg's set is similar to that which he played in Tallinn. Except that he makes a rather oblique remark about the need for us all to become vegetarians: this, in fact, is a little in-joke aimed at discomposing the likes of Sasha Voronkow and the poetess/prostate masseuse. A central part of their script was that everyone should be kind to animals, a notion that as yet seems

rather alien in the Soviet Union – from experience I can say that it's difficult to be a vegetarian in the Soviet Union.

Billy begins each show with Marvin Gaye's 'I Heard It Through The Grapevine', then plays a good half-hour's-worth of his own material, concluding with a rendition of "that old English folk-song, The Clash's 'Garageland'." Again, he provides lengthy introductions which are translated by Ultravox Sasha from a table and microphone in the photographers' pit. And the song that is greeted with the most applause is the one whose introduction contains the line, "This could easily apply to the youth of the Soviet Union," – 'Help Save The Youth Of America'. (When, a few months later, a live version of this song, recorded in the USSR and complete with translated introduction, is released in the USA as a single, it is widely ignored by the media, as though on some paranoid point of principle.)

At each show Billy Bragg receives a more than excellent reception, one that would appear to justify the tapes being rolled by a Melodia engineer at the mixing desk for what Bragg discovers is a live album that the state record company intends to release in the USSR. "It would be nice," remarks manager Peter Jenner wryly, "if they'd ask us if they could do it first."

But the overwhelming applause is reserved for Aquarium's mixture of modern and traditional music, played with modern and traditional instrumentation. The greatest cheers of all come for the combination of Aquarium and Billy Bragg, along with Bravo and the 'Una Paloma Blanca'-style duck people, performing Peter Tosh's 'Get Up, Stand Up'. It would seem that a larger proportion of this audience went to see UB40 on their tour of the USSR than will be going to see Uriah Heep.

Discussing Cultural Imperialism on Arbat Street, Moscow.

At eight o'clock the next morning photographer Adrian Boot is awoken by Billy knocking on the door of his bedroom at the Hotel Ukraine. Bragg, who is often insomniac, has noticed that for the first time since we arrived there is a clear blue sky above Moscow, and knows that the light is almost perfect for a good photo session. Though perhaps not motivated entirely by altruism – Bragg fully understands the meaning of the rock 'n' roll pose – such a gesture of co-operation from a popular musician is so removed from the norm that revealing it here may well result in Billy Bragg being struck off by the Musicians' Union.

O n the Saturday night Billy and his party have been invited to dinner at the home of a married couple who are two of the Soviet Union's leading intellectual journalists and rock fans. This is set to take place after that evening's shows. Accordingly, at a quarter to midnight, we find ourselves dropped off from the Intourist bus at the subway station entrance by Red Square. We have already encountered this subway station earlier in the day, on a brief visit to the nearby GUM store. A pair of black marketeers, looking remarkably unlike the super-spiv part played by Alexei Sayle in the film of *Gorky Park*, had accosted us and made a date to arrive at our hotel later that afternoon, loaded with barterable booty. Clearly cool cats, both wore their rabbit-skin fur hats with the ear-flaps hanging loose and untied, a sort of Soviet equivalent of the home-boy fashion of wearing basketball sneakers with the laces undone. They did not wear these hats for long, however: they were soon exchanged for assorted U2, Talking Heads, and even Billy Bragg cassettes – only top quality artists accepted. Bragg also scored an official, and slightly smelly, ice-hockey player's shirt bearing the colours and position

GUM department store, great architecture, shame about the shops.

number of one of Moscow's ranking teams. And a number of intricately hand-painted, delicate wooden boxes were also bought by Billy Bragg and myself. Throughout their time in our hotel our black marketeer friends spoke only in English, not even acknowledging any Russian being spoken around them.

Anyway, accompanied this time by Peter Jenner, the Billy Bragg posse is down in the tube station at midnight, a point that Bragg and Wiggy certainly do not lose the opportunity to make. But these Moscow subway stations are quite different to those Paul Weller wrote about. In fact, they give the impression of having been hacked from hunks of marble, as though these Stalinist monuments are intended to be public showcases of the might and majesty of the Soviet Union. And they are works of great aesthetic beauty. There is not an ounce of litter on display on the stations nor on the train that we board. But we do spot piles of puke by a couple of supporting pillars, indications surely that Gorbachev's efforts to stamp out drunkenness have not been a total success.

Get ahead get a hat.

A very long way from Barking.

Like excited schoolboys on an away-day pass we board the spotless train, Adrian Boot immediately turning it into a moving studio for shooting a succession of pictures of Billy wearing various funny hats. The train is at least half-full. But, as was the experience of Clint Eastwood – who we closely resemble – in the film *Firefox* when he rode the Moscow subway, no one pays us the least attention. There are 160 other languages, apart from Russian, spoken in the USSR, so we are no doubt assumed to be speaking some curious Baltic tongue.

With us is our guide, Ultravox Sasha. When, as we can tell from the subway map, we are in the far reaches of the Moscow suburbs, he tells us that the next station is our stop. By now the train is no longer travelling underground. Outside, for some time, all we have seen is mile after mile of frozen wasteland *Clockwork Orange*-land. It looks rather cold.

If the hat fits wear it.

It is extremely cold. There seems to be no wind whatsoever, as the full moon is reflected on the glistening ice-packs of snow through which narrow footpaths have been established: this is very dissimilar to the centre of Moscow where armies of immensely efficient snow-clearers are constantly in action.

And it is some walk from the station to the home of our hosts. Our ears, fingers, toes, and noses experience intense pain: the temperature is around minus 15 degrees centigrade. Then we discover we are lost.

There do not appear to be any names or numbers on any of the low-rise apartment blocks we check out, stumbling from snowdrift to snowdrift, and trying, unsuccessfully, to avoid tumbling on the ice. After a quarter of an hour or so it is not really much fun any more. Cowardly, the English party decides to shelter in the doorway of an apartment block; meanwhile, the Russian speakers are sent ahead to try and find precisely where we are meant to be going.

While we are waiting for them to return Billy Bragg pushes the door to the block. It opens. He steps inside. We follow.

Inside there is warmth. A lot of warmth. It billows up from the boiler that heats the block, sited just around the corner of the flight of stone steps that leads into the basement. There is also the reassuring discovery that communal areas in Soviet apartment blocks stink of piss just like they do in Britain.

We 'hunker down', as American magazine writers would describe our postures, luxuriating in the sudden warmth. For whatever reasons, we embark on a discussion about Peter Wright's *Spycatcher* book. After some minutes Billy Bragg points out that if, at half-past midnight on a Saturday night, an English tenant of a London tower block found himself in the basement of his flats and discovered a party of Russian-speaking fellows, wearing western military insignia and giggling insanely, there could well arise something of an international incident.

Finally, however, our Russian guides reappear: the flat has been found. Moscow flats are (almost predictably) rather like those of Manhattan: small and, by necessity, neatly ordered. And this is no exception: it has a small kitchen, an adequate living-room, and a pair of bedrooms, in one of which – the couple's daughter's – may be found a Soviet copy, on the Melodia label, of the first Whitney Houston LP.

The atmosphere is at first rather formal. But then small, decorated glasses of vodka are filled and handed round. A toast is called: the Western contingent sip wimpishly at their drinks until they are shown how pathetic they are being: the man from *Construction News* flings the drink down his throat in one gulp (he also performs a little trick in which he places the entire glass in his mouth . . .). We are instructed to do similarly. Then there is another toast, just to get us in practice, as it were. WHAM! down the hatch. Suddenly everyone begins to act in a rather animated manner.

Svengali ★ *Peter Jenner.*

In stark contrast to the food we have been served over the last few days in Soviet restaurants, this meal is a gourmet's delight. No bread queues in this household: blinis, carp, every possible variety of cheese, sour cream, herring, a mixture of fresh vegetables. The meal, we are told, is a combination of Georgian and Russian Jewish dishes – our hostess is Jewish.

For at least three hours we sit at the table. In innumerable toasts, bottle after bottle of vodka is consumed with a gusto like that of children with access to a crate of 'pop'. Somewhere towards the end of the evening, by which time the serpentine meanderings of sozzled conversation have drawn us from the table to perch uncertainly on the edge of chairs and stools about the room, the subject of private education is raised.

Essentially, Billy Bragg, backed up by Peter Jenner, the evil **Svengali** of pop, is having a go at Adrian Boot and myself: both us hapless hacks refuse to dismiss out-of-hand the idea of educating our children privately if we feel that what the State provides is woefully inadequate – we will not, we state with a measure of satisfied self-righteousness, play ideological games with our children's futures. Suddenly, support comes from an unexpected quarter: oh yes, says Ultravox Sasha, he would do exactly the same for his children; and, he adds, by way of emphasis, he wouldn't have the job he has today if, throughout his childhood, his parents hadn't paid for regular private foreign language tuition.

Bragg and Jenner momentarily appear like men who have discovered that the entire premises of their existence have been built on sandy ground. Boot and I suddenly become blood-brothers with Sasha: arrangements are made to send large boxes of Lego for his children as soon as we return to Britain. In the half-light of dawn we travel the long taxi journey back to our hotel together, basking in a glow of smugness, that is only matched by the aura of righteousness emanating from Bragg and Jenner.

The next morning we all feel dreadful. Wiggy, who had somehow ended up sitting in the kitchen with our host, ironing out the creases in the Warsaw Pact, is inevitably the worst off. He is unable to speak until around five in the afternoon.

Although the sun is again shining, the temperature outside is around -15. All the same, it is decided that a further photo session will take place, in the environs of Red Square. We contemplate going to look at Lenin's tomb, but, as always, a good two hours' queueing would be involved. Deliberating over this for only a moment or two we find our feet are already in pain from the cold; although Billy makes jokes about being on the guest-list, the idea is dropped. I ask him what he thinks to the Russian rock 'n' roll groups he has seen.

"Well, some of them seem a bit too much into the heavy rock scene – too much stuck right in the centre of things. That seems to be what most of

Queuing to view Lenin's mausoleum in Red Square.

Lenin the famous cat lover.

Lenin ⭐ *Considered something of a saint in the Soviet Union, and very popular, with the youth as well as adults. No longer a historical figure, but part of mythology. Lenin is the principle icon of the Soviet Union. Very popular in trendy western artwork.*

Karl Marx ⭐ *This German Jew probably had no idea that his books would lead to sit-ins in universities throughout the West in the late 1960s, or that they would help create the*

them are drawn to, which has never attracted me in the least. The more interesting ones are the experimental ones. Unfortunately, because we don't understand their lyrics, we don't know exactly what they're singing about. But there are quite a few, ones who're working outside the constrictions of Melodia and the official rock clubs, who seem to have an interesting edge. I get the feeling that the rock 'n' roll clubs have been put there simply to control the rock 'n' roll that is going on rather than to make it more interesting."

I was shocked when I learned yesterday that the groups on the bill with you are being paid 20 roubles a show, which is about 20 pounds.

"Yes. And the market is so huge. You're talking about millions and millions of punters out there buying Aquarium and Bravo records. They're not even receiving 10 per cent of what a Western act would earn for the same sort of sales."

It seems an absolute disgrace, I say, as we pass the gates of the Kremlin.

"Yes. But the alternative is sitting at home on your butt making cassettes. At least if you're in Bravo you might get a chance to go and play abroad. There's an incredible compromise they have to make just to do things we take absolutely for granted, just so they can go and play abroad and buy some decent equipment."

Do you think this can actually be sorted out: the fact that all these acts are being stitched up by the state-owned record company Melodia?

"Everyone else in this country is getting stitched up. I don't see why the pop stars should be any different from everybody else. But it's the sort of dead hand of bureaucracy, isn't it? It just shows what rubbish it is when people in England rabbit on about nationalising the record industry: now you see what happens if records are made by committees. It's just stupid. So obviously, in some way the Soviet music business must become more

independent. Which it only can at the moment through the release of home-made cassettes and the like. But the people at Melodia want to control everything. So I don't think that for the moment very much is going to change."

Who do you consider are the greats that have influenced you?

"The greats? Well, **Lenin, Karl Marx, Bertold Brecht, Batman** . . . I don't know: **Hank Williams, Robert Johnson** – where's *he* now. Nobody even knows who he is any more."

How old were you when you got into such notions as Lenin?

"Well, it wasn't really a question of getting into the notion of it. You kind of learn as you go along, don't you? Needless to say, I never learnt anything about it whatsoever at school. I'm chipping away at little bits of Lenin and really still trying to put him in a historical context. But coming over here really whets your curiosity, and you start to find out more and more

worst restaurants in the world. Actually, a bit of a frightful person – drunk, treated family terribly, boils on bum from all those years sitting in the British Museum library – but rather important. This is despite the fact that he is a very boring writer: this is the reason no-one has read his books, although a lot of people pretend to have done – they are unreadable. The one thing you can always get in bookshops in any socialist country is books on Karl Marx: this is because they are not page-turning, rattling reads and there are no dirty bits.

Berthold Brecht ★ *In the same way that Karl Marx is the most important political writer of the nineteenth century though no-one has read him, Berthold Brecht is the most important dramatist of the twentieth century, though no-one has seen his plays if they can possibly avoid them. Actually, if you study him and really get stuck into that whole Brechtian thing he's fantastic: great visuals – all that theatre-in-the-round, non-proscenium arch stuff all started with Bert.*

81

Hank Williams ★ *The greatest country singer that ever lived. Composer of 'Your Cheating Heart', 'I Saw The Light' and 'I'm So Lonesome I Could Cry' amongst others. Died prematurely of self-abuse on January 1, 1953.*

Robert Johnson ★ *Arguably the greatest black blues artist of them all. Alleged to have entered a Faustian pact with the devil in exchange for extraordinary prowess on the guitar. Composer of 'Crossroads', 'Rambling On My Mind' and 'Love In Vain', amongst others. Huge influence on all subsequent black and white blues guitarists. Died in mysterious circumstances in August, 1938.*

Batman ★ *Surreal law-enforcer of Gotham City, aka Bruce Wayne, millionaire philanthropist. With side-kick Robin, fought against such brilliant criminal minds as The Joker, The Riddler and Catwoman on long running, recently rediscovered T.V. series from the sixties.*

about subjects like Lenin – there's only so much they bother to tell you in history books.

"For example, I never really understood about the whole cult of Lenin – that he's considered not just as a personality, but as an icon. But like most Russian heroes, the unfortunate prerequisite is that you must be dead. Because dead men can't actually turn round and criticize things. But they've always been big on icons in the Soviet Union – they really seem to need them. And they've kind of replaced the icon of the Tsar, the father of all the Russians, with Lenin. He's now their icon, the picture they look at all the time.

"What can I tell you, Christopher? It is freezing, ain't it? Did you know I've got two pairs of thermals on?"

I've only got one pair on.

We wander past the glory of St. Basil's cathedral. ("They certainly know their onions," quips Bragg, pointing to the circular domes scattered about the top of the building), and then down to the banks of the Moskva, which is one snaking lump of thick ice. All around us factories spew out polluted smoke, one of the images that turned Stalin on most, as is pointed out by the bard of Barking (very sic).

Nearby is evidence that the peculiar (lack of) aesthetic vision was not limited to J. Stalin: in fact, a general lack of taste and sensitivity seems to have been a characteristic of every Soviet régime until Gorbachev came along – with Lenin, Gorbachev shares the distinction of having been the only Soviet

St. Basils, Red Square.

be the old thinking. Still, it must be very frustrating for them. But there is a little bit of reform going on, and let's hope it gives them enough to keep persevering at it."

Well, Gorbachev wants the Soviet Union to be a totally post-industrial society by the year 2,000.

"He's got a job on his hands, hasn't he? Hasn't he indeed. Well, you know, it's going to be a long, fast, scary trip for all you folks out there in the Soviet Union. So I'd hold on tight if I were you."

We bid farewell to the Finns, who are returning that night to Helsinki. The journey to the station on the Intourist bus is subdued, as much from sadness at leaving Moscow as from exhaustion.

On the platform of the Leningrad station, the snow is partially melted. We board the 1.00pm express to Leningrad, after warm hugs of genuine friendship from Sacha and Sacha (the well-known Socialist advertising agency). The long train pulls out of the station. Bragg pulls on an eye-mask, and, tucked away at the rear of the plane-style seats, falls asleep. One can't help reflecting on how these Soviet train journeys seem a logical extension of the first Bragg image: the highly mobile, rockin' singer-songwriter taking

Sleep is the enemy.

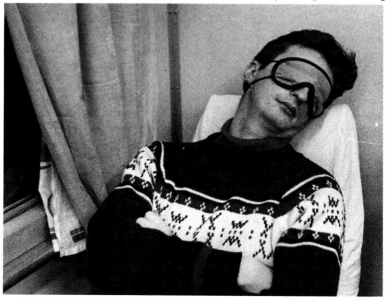

British Rail 125s to shows, armed only with a portable amp and his cheap Arbiter Les Paul-copy guitar.

When he wakes, it is to the sound of one of his own tunes – 'Richard' – blaring out of the carriage's speaker system. Peter Jenner has befriended the two women whose job it is to care for our carriage, and given them a cassette of 'Taxman'. Bragg immediately swings into heavy badge-swapping mode, before we retire to the restaurant car. Wiggy remains behind in the carriage, listening on a Walkman to a compilation tape he has made of various Faces and early Rod Stewart LPs – formative influences on himself and Bragg, as they should be for any discerning rock 'n' roller.

The food in the restaurant car seems like an offering from the gods compared with what had been presented to us so often in Moscow: we eat fish soup, and a mixture of potatoes and vegetables at a price of 80 pence each – we compare this with the £15.00 or so we would have been charged in a British Rail restaurant car.

We arrive in Leningrad at 10.00 in the evening, and get a taxi to our hotel. On the way, we drive past the exterior of the Winter Palace, and are staggered by its beauty. Our hotel is sited opposite the battleship Aurora, from which the shot that signalled the beginning of the October revolution was fired. But in our hotel, another sort of revolution is taking place: the package holiday revolution.

It is a very different institution from the Hotel Ukraine in Moscow. Here one hears the distinctive tones, familiar in many foreign situations, of middle-aged, middle-class English, tetchy that details of life in Leningrad are

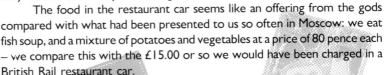

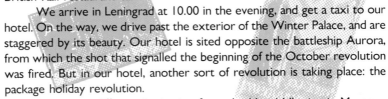

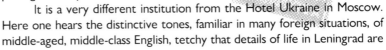

Leningrad concert.

not precisely as they are in their suburban hometowns. Here one hears Dutch and German, and the various Scandinavian tongues in action. Here, inevitably, are parties of Finns, getting drunk. We go to sleep.

Quite unusually for the USSR, the next morning is formidably cold. Much of it is spent in book and poster shops, although for some time Wiggy and myself stamp our frozen feet on the equally frozen pavement outside the Winter Palace as Billy Bragg takes part in a final Adrian Boot photo-session.

At eight o'clock that evening Billy Bragg performs his final concert in the Soviet Union at the small Leningrad rock club. Several members of Aquarium are present in an audience that seems far hipper, in its general Beat sensibility, than that at the Moscow Olympic weight-lifting hall. This is not surprising: this Bragg show is in that long rock 'n' roll tradition of prestige 'secret' gigs. And so this is a very 'cool' audience, with obligatory drunken punks backstage.

All the same, when Billy attempts, in one of his lengthy song introductions, to have the word 'yuppie' translated into Russian, communication breaks down. "Oh well," he mutters in an aside to Peter Jenner, "a little more perestroika and they'll know." As I note this down, in my seat in the front row of the audience, Bragg steps off the stage, still playing his Arbiter, and bellows, laughing, "Don't write that down and make it the whole point of what you're saying, you bastard!"

The evening ends with what used to be known in the sixties as a 'jam' session, with the various members of Aquarium, Wiggy, and the drunken punks, performing an array of classic rock 'n' roll songs.

After the show, we go to Boris Grebenschikov's Leningrad apartment. This appears like something straight out of Dostoevsky, a mildew-encrusted large flat, five floors up a vast communal stairwell bespattered with graffiti from Aquarium fans. The feeling about it is distinctly like that of a London squat – appropriately enough, because that is what it apparently is. Boris Grebenschikov, his wife, and three-month old baby have only one room in this magnificent old place which, slapbang in the centre of Leningrad, would in any capitalist country have been delightedly seized upon by property developers.

The Wailers play on a cassette deck as the inevitable bottles of vodka are produced, along with bars of chocolate. On the walls are icons and vaguely mystical paintings. As soon as the vodka begins to be consumed the marginally morose atmosphere disappears, to be replaced by a state of great animation. Two or three of the Russians present become almost paralytically drunk; it is when they get into such a state that they attempt to draw you into hopeless attempts at deep and meaningful discussion. At one point, I realise, there are *four* separate conversations taking place about The Clash. Appropriately, one of the two punks present passes out on the sofa. Very late indeed we return to our hotel.

At Boris's flat.

The next morning we take the hour-long drive out to the airport. Here, the old thinking is certainly on display. Despite the fact that Billy Bragg has played in the Soviet Union for free, the woman at the check-in desk demands an immense amount of money because of the excess baggage situation created by Billy's equipment. When we get into the departure lounge we realise that Aeroflot has managed to approximately double the revenue on our flight through this additional charge: apart from an elderly couple, we are the only passengers booked on to the plane – perestroika notwithstanding, flights to the West are not yet a growth industry in the Soviet Union.

СВЕРХ УСТАНОВЛЕННОЙ НОРМЫ БЕСПЛАТНОГО ПРОВОЗА БАГАЖА МОЖНО БЕСПЛАТНО ПРОВОЗИТЬ СЛЕДУЮЩИЕ ПРЕДМЕТЫ, ЕСЛИ ОНИ НАХО-ДЯТСЯ НА РУКАХ У ПАССАЖИРА И НЕ ВЛОЖЕНЫ В БАГАЖ:

FOR YOUR AIR TRIP THE FOLLOWING ARTICLES WHEN RETAINED IN YOUR CUSTODY WILL BE CARRIED FREE OVER AND ABOVE THE FREE BAGGAGE ALLOWANCE:

ДАМСКАЯ СУМОЧКА ИЛИ ПАПКА ДЛЯ БУМАГ	ПЕЧАТНЫЕ ИЗДАНИЯ ДЛЯ ЧТЕНИЯ В ПОЛЁТЕ	ПИТАНИЕ ДЛЯ РЕБЁНКА И ДЕТСКАЯ ДОРОЖНАЯ КОЛЫБЕЛЬКА	ЗОНТИК ИЛИ ТРОСТЬ	ПАЛЬТО ИЛИ ПЛАЩ	СКЛАДНАЯ ИНВАЛИДНАЯ КОЛЯСКА И/ИЛИ КОСТЫЛИ, ЕСЛИ ТАКИЕ ПРЕДМЕТЫ ПАССАЖИРУ НЕОБХОДИМЫ
ONE LADY'S HANDBAG OR PAPER CASE	A REASONABLE AMOUNT OF READING MATTER FOR THE FLIGHT	INFANT'S FOOD FOR CONSUMPTION IN FLIGHT AND INFANT'S CARRYING BASKET	ONE UMBRELLA OR WALKING STICK	ONE OVERCOAT OR WRAP ONE BLANKET	A FULLY COLLAPSIBLE INVALID'S WHEEL CHAIR AND/OR A PAIR OF CRUTCHES PROVIDED THAT THE PASSENGER IS DEPENDENT ON THEM

ДЕТСКАЯ КОЛЫБЕЛЬКА, ИНВАЛИДНАЯ КОЛЯСКА И КОСТЫЛИ МОГУТ ПРОВОЗИТЬСЯ В БАГАЖНОМ ОТДЕЛЕНИИ САМОЛЁТА

THE INFANT'S CARRYING BASKET, THE WHEEL CHAIR AND THE PAIR OF CRUTCHES MAY ALSO BE CARRIED IN THE CARGO COMPARTMENT.

Before this transpires, however, there has been a moment of tension as we pass through customs: bags are searched both coming into *and* leaving the Soviet Union. Unwisely, Billy has left a Russian army cap at the top of his bag: this is immediately confiscated, and, inevitably, everyone else's bags are then assiduously gone through. We note that there are, in fact, more customs men than there are passengers on our flight, a classic example of Soviet underemployment.

Three-and-a-half hours later our TV 134 arrows down to the runway at Amsterdam's Schipol airport. The first thing we see as the plane lands – before it has even touched down on the runway, in fact – is a neon advertising hoarding for **Sony**.

Sony ★ *Where would we be without Sony Walkmans? What the Soviet citizens want more than anything else is loads of Japanese consumer durables, which is a great new market for the Japanese.*

Вы сделали хороший выбор!
Аэрофлот предлагает прекрасные
условия для деловых и туристических
путешествий, гарантирует комфорт и
гостеприимство.
Благодарим за полет!

You have made a good choice!
Aeroflot offers you excellent conditions
for business and tourist trips,
guaranteeing comfort and hospitality.
Thank you for the flight!

DISCOGRAPHY

This is not a complete discography but lists all the main releases to date.

BILLY BRAGG
ALBUMS

**LIFE'S A RIOT
WITH SPY VS SPY**
Utility Records. Util 1
Released July 1, 1983
Go! Discs. Util 1
Re-released November 1983

**BREWING UP
WITH BILLY BRAGG**
Go! Discs. AGOLP 4
Released October 4, 1984

**TALKING WITH THE
TAXMAN ABOUT POETRY**
Go! Discs. AGOLP 6
Released September 22, 1986
CD: AGOCD 6
Released June 1, 1987

THE PEEL SESSIONS
Strange Fruit Records. SFPS 027
Recorded July 27, 1983.
Transmitted August 3, 1983
Released 1987

**BACK TO BASICS
WITH BILLY BRAGG ★**
Go! Discs. AGOLP 8
Released June 1, 1987
CD: AGOCD 8

WORKERS PLAYTIME
Go! Discs. AGOLP 15
Released September 19, 1988
CD: AGOCD 15

SINGLES

**Between The Wars
Which Side Are You On
World Turned Upside Down
It Says Here**
Go! Discs EP. AGOEP 1
Released February 28,1985

**Days Like These
I Don't Need This
   Pressure Ron
Scholarship Is The Enemy
   Of Romance**
Go! Discs. GOD 8. GOD X 8.12″
Released December 12, 1985

**St. Swithin's Day
A New England**
Double A European. 107067
Germany -100, France AE140
Released 1986

**Levi Stubbs' Tears
Think Again
Walk Away Renée version**
Go! Discs. GOD 12
**Levi Stubbs' Tears
Between The Wars Live
Think Again
Walk Away Renée version**
Go! Discs. GOD X12. 12″
Released June 12, 1986

**Greetings To The New
   Brunette
The Tatler**
Go! Discs. GOD 15
**Greetings To The New
   Brunette
Deportees
The Tatler
Jeane
There Is Power In A Union**
Go! Discs. GOD X15. 12″
Released November 3, 1986

**Help Save The Youth Of
   America
Think Again
Chile Your Waters Run Red
   Through Soweto
Days Like These
To Have And To Have Not
There Is Power In A Union**
Live – 12″/CD/Cass. single
(USA and Canada only)
Elektra 9 60787-1
Released April 15, 1988

**Waiting For The Great
   Leap Forwards
Wishing The Days Away
Sin City**
Go! Discs. GOD 23
Released August 22, 1988

**She's Got A New Spell
Must I Paint You A Picture**
Go! Discs. GOD 24
Released November 14, 1988

★ Back To Basics companion
LP song book, minus two songs.
Available from record and book
shops or by post: Express Music,
PO Box 153,London WC2H OLD
Music published by Warner/
Chappell Music Ltd. London
Sincere Management:
Flat B, 6 Bravington Road,
London W9 3AH
Go! Discs: 320-322 King Street,
Hammersmith, London W6 0RR